ESSENTIALS
of Licensing
Intellectual Property

Essentials Series

The Essentials Series was created for busy business advisory and corporate professionals. The books in this series were designed so that these busy professionals can quickly acquire knowledge and skills in core business areas.

Each book provides need-to-have fundamentals for those professionals who must:

- Get up to speed quickly, because they have been promoted to a new position or have broadened their responsibility scope
- Manage a new functional area
- Brush up on new developments in their area of responsibility
- Add more value to their company or clients

Other books in this series include:

For more information on any of the above titles, please visit *www.wiley.com*.

ESSENTIALS
of Licensing
Intellectual Property

Alexander I. Poltorak
Paul J. Lerner

WILEY

John Wiley & Sons, Inc.

Published by John Wiley & Sons, Inc., Hoboken, New Jersey
Published simultaneously in Canada

For general information on our other products and services, or technical support, please contact our Customer Care Department within the United States at 800-762-2974, outside the United States at 317-572-3993 or fax 317-572-4002.

Wiley also publishes its books in a variety of electronic formats. Some content that appears in print may not be available in electronic books.

For more information about Wiley products, visit our web site at *www.wiley.com*.

Library of Congress Cataloging-in-Publication Data:

ISBN 978-0-471-43233-3

10   9   8

About the Authors

Alexander I. Poltorak is the founder and chief executive officer of General Patent Corporation (GPC), an intellectual property (IP) management company focusing on patent licensing and enforcement, international technology transfer, and IP portfolio management. Prior to establishing GPC in 1989, Dr. Poltorak was the president of Poltorak Associates Inc., a management consulting and patent licensing firm, which he formed in 1987. Before that he was chief executive officer of Rapitech Systems, Inc., a publicly traded computer company that he cofounded in 1983. Prior to Rapitech, Dr. Poltorak served as Assistant Professor of Biomathematics at the Neurology Department of Cornell University Medical College, where he conducted research in image processing and computer tomography. He also served as Assistant Professor of Physics at Touro College. Dr. Poltorak has published several papers in scientific journals.

Dr. Poltorak emigrated from the former USSR in 1982, where he was awarded a doctorate in physics at the age of 22 for a significant breakthrough in Einstein's Theory of Relativity. As a political dissident, he was later stripped of his degrees for anticommunist activities. He is a member of the Licensing Executives Society (LES), the Association of University Technology Managers (AUTM), Intellectual Property Owners Association (IPO), the National Association of Corporate Directors, the New York Academy of Science, and the American Physical Society. He was a US co-chairman for the Subcommittee on Information Exchange of the US-USSR Trade and Economic Counsel. He is on the advisory board of *Patent Strategy & Management*, for which he cowrote

"Corporate Officers and Directors Can Be Liable for Mismanaging Intellectual Property." The article appeared in its May and June 2000 issues. He is coauthor with attorney Paul J. Lerner of an article about *Grain Processing v. American Maize Products*, "Grain, Grain, Go Away," which examines recent major developments in lost profits. The article appeared in the February 2000 edition of *Intellectual Property Worldwide*. In June of 2000 Dr. Poltorak delivered a lecture on technology transfer from Russia at the International Technology Transfer Seminar organized by the American Conference Institute.

Paul J. Lerner is the senior vice president and general counsel of General Patent Corporation (GPC), an intellectual property (IP) management company focusing on patent licensing and enforcement, international technology transfer, and IP portfolio management. Before joining GPC, Mr. Lerner was a partner in the Hartford, Connecticut, business law firm of Pepe & Hazard LLP. He has led IP law departments at Olin Corporation, Black & Decker Corporation, and multinational electrical construction giant Asea Brown Boveri, Inc.

Prior to embarking on a law career, Mr. Lerner was a project manager at the Illinois Institute of Technology Research Institute in Chicago, where he managed a technology transfer and technology forecasting team. Mr. Lerner's education includes a BS in Aeronautical Engineering from Purdue University, an MBA from Loyola University, a JD from DePaul University, and postgraduate legal studies at John Marshall College of Law. He is an adjunct professor of IP law at the University of New Haven.

Mr. Lerner is a member of the Licensing Executives Society (LES) and the American Intellectual Property Law Association (AIPLA). He is coauthor with GPC's chairman and CEO, Alexander I. Poltorak, of an article about *Grain Processing v. American Maize Products*, "Grain, Grain, Go Away," which examined recent major developments in lost profits.

The article appeared in the February 2000 edition of *Intellectual Property Worldwide*. He also cowrote "Corporate Officers and Directors Can Be Liable for Mismanaging Intellectual Property," which appeared in the May and June 2000 issues of *Patent Strategy & Management*. In September 2000 Mr. Lerner's article "Strategic Auditing: The Key to Minimizing Litigation Bills" was published by *corporateintelligence.com*.

General Patent Corporation is based in Montebello Park, Suffern, New York, and has offices in Hungary, Russia, and Israel.

Contents

Contents

Foreword

The invention of e-mail as an efficient mode of communication gives rise to an intriguing benefit: One need not answer a question immediately as would be expected in real-time conversation. Therefore, on occasion, I prefer to ponder before I answer, as I did when honored with the request to write this preface to *Essentials of Licensing Intellectual Property*.

My initial response was to decline, stating that I was too busy to read yet another licensing book. Honestly, I really am too busy to plow through more theoretical jargon. Too busy to pull out my calculator to analyze complex royalty or valuation models. Too busy to hear one more author sell me more pixie dust that magically turns patents into winning lottery tickets.

As we have all witnessed in the recent past, countless books on licensing IP have been written as best-seller novels to excite the soul and incite a spark of larceny; maps that we should follow to discover long-forgotten patent treasures that await discovery and exploitation.

Other patent licensing treatises are excellent examples of IP consultants and theorists attempting to explain the complexity of IP law and the mystical process of extracting value (money) from idle IP assets; ultimately these works leave the reader feeling lost and helpless, believing that hiring a consultant is the only way to profit from their unexploited IP.

I also felt that you, the reader, have lost your appetite for another helping of licensing leftovers, too full of IP licensing prophesy to gulp down yet another spoonful. Fortunately, this was one of those occasions that I paused to contemplate.

Why? Because I owed it to two of the IP industry's most respected realists, Alexander Poltorak and Paul Lerner, and to the business and investment communities, to evaluate whether these authors could merge their contemporary legal expertise with recognized firsthand licensing success to create a hands-on IP licensing reference.

After reading and reflecting on this book, I clicked "reply" on my e-mail and accepted their kind invitation.

This book is a fast, friendly, insightful read—I couldn't put it down, and consumed it cover to cover in a single sitting (except for a few quick trips to refill my diet soda).

You'll want to read *Essentials of Licensing Intellectual Property* for the same reason you read any book on licensing . . . it's a guide to generating money. But while other books on licensing espouse a process to make fast money, *Essentials of Licensing Intellectual Property* is an easy-to-use tool that empowers you to become a fast learner on how to generate revenue and increase shareholder value—not only from patents, but also from trademarks, copyrights, mask works, and more.

IP management is a serious business in which fortunes can be made or lost quickly. Managers of IP are held accountable to shareholders, with the new financial accounting standards now requiring line-item reporting of IP value. Interestingly, though, Poltorak and Lerner kept me laughing throughout the book. Their storytelling style and tongue-in-cheek euphemisms not only keep this book flowing quickly, but they burn the most important concepts indelibly into the reader's mind.

It's light, but deep. It's an overview, but it also clearly outlines the steps necessary to build a profitable IP strategy and deploy smart licensing tactics. It's full of pointed tips and helpful advice that can empower any manager to quickly obtain a solid, hands-on working knowledge of the essentials of IP licensing. (Maybe that's why it's the title of the book.)

Applicable to experienced and new MBAs, read this book and by the end of the day, you'll understand how to build traction for your IP licensing strategy, enhancing your company's most valuable and sustainable competitive advantage, its IP!

Managers, investors, and shareholders will quickly develop a meaningful vocabulary and understanding of the essential legal and business elements involved in IP licensing—and the incredible value that can be realized if sensible management is applied to this licensing process.

Even experienced licensing professionals, who have become victims of their own proclivity to migrate clear IP licensing objectives toward complex licensing agreements, will find *Essentials of Licensing Intellectual Property* to be a timely, snappy refresher.

If you're looking for an ivory-tower book that will allow you to impress the executive staff with your expansive but instant knowledge of IP licensing theory and mastery of complex IP valuation models, buy a different book. But if your objective is to gain an immediate command of the practicalities of licensing IP assets, Poltorak and Lerner have given you everything you need to hit the ground running by Monday morning.

Although e-mail brought the promise of instant communication, I wonder if it was ever envisioned as a method to pause and reflect before continuing with the dialogue. This time, at least, I'm glad I did. For insightful books like this, I'll never be too busy!

Andy Gibbs
CEO, PatentCafe.com, Inc.
Coauthor, *Essentials of Patents*
Second-term member, USPTO Public Patent Advisory Committee
Board of Directors, Intellectual Property Owners Association

Preface

Of late, much has been written about intellectual property (IP) and how it forms the modern basis for wealth. Readers are advised to create intellectual property, by stimulating its generation and securing its legal protection. They are advised to search their organizations for undiscovered or "hidden" intellectual property, to "audit," "mine," and "triage" their IP. Yet all of this effort, directed to the creation of intellectual property or the identification of existing property, does not in itself yield wealth.

Intellectual property is not wealth; it is a tool that, properly used, will *produce* wealth. The potential wealth that IP represents is locked away and is unlocked only when the property is utilized in the production of goods or services for sale in the market. Such utilization, of course, may be by the creator of the intellectual property. Yet often the IP creator is unable to utilize it, to utilize it effectively, or to utilize it to its fullest extent. In such circumstances, the property owner may assign (sell) the property to a party better situated to its employ. Many IP owners, however, are reluctant or unwilling to sell it. Owners may, for example, wish to retain the right to use the property themselves, either in the present or in the future. Moreover, it may be difficult or impossible to find a buyer willing and able to pay the price an IP owner deems appropriate. How then is the owner to fully realize the potential value of the property? The answer, of course, is licensing. The owner of intellectual property may realize its value by licensing it to one or more parties who will utilize it in the creation of goods and services. For all of the obvious importance of licensing, little attention has been directed to it, and many business executives remain ignorant of its principles, its pitfalls, and the opportunities it may present. This book discusses the basic issues of licensing and the effective conversion of IP into real wealth.

Chapter 1 defines licensing, explains its advantages, and sets forth principles for selecting those properties to be licensed and those to be abandoned. Chapter 2 introduces the reader to the basic rules of contract law, including the elements of a contract and the general structure of a license. Chapter 3 provides a primer of the various types of intellectual property—the subject of any license. Licensing strategies are discussed in Chapter 4.

The book next addresses the particular issues involved in the licensing of patents, know-how and trade secrets, trademarks, and copyrights (Chapters 5 through 8, respectively). In Chapter 9, the different roles of the "paid-up" and "running royalty" licenses are discussed, as well as the factors that determine royalty rates. Chapter 10 addresses the policing and enforcement of licenses, from the viewpoint of both licensor and licensee. Finally, Chapter 11 deals with negotiation, addressing negotiation skills and the rules for a successful negotiation. Chapter 11 is followed by Appendices A–K and a list of suggested further reading.

Authors' Note

The purpose of this book is to introduce business executives and inventors to the principles underlying the licensing of intellectual property in the business environment. The book describes key concepts and facts, and illustrates how these concepts and facts should influence decision making. Of necessity, these descriptions are generalized.

Exceptions abound to every rule stated in the following chapters. (Your lawyer will be more than happy to enumerate these exceptions for you.) Moreover, the law is a living, constantly evolving creature. The rules of the game are constantly changing—often in midplay and sometimes retroactively. A little knowledge is a dangerous thing. Before making important decisions, review matters with a qualified professional. Reading this book, however carefully, is no substitute for professional guidance.

The authors wish to thank Susan McDermott of John Wiley & Sons, Inc., for her patience and unfailing enthusiasm for this book. We are also grateful to Nava Cooper for preparing the manuscript for publication and to Lisa Meyers for her help with typing the manuscript.

ESSENTIALS

of Licensing
Intellectual Property

CHAPTER 1

Introduction

 After reading this chapter you will be able to

- Understand what a license is
- Understand why a license may be desirable
- Know how to choose which intellectual property to license and which to abandon

Background

What a License Is

A license is, simply stated, permission to do something the granting party (the licensor) has the right to otherwise prohibit. In the context of intellectual property (IP) licensing, it is a grant, by the owner of the property, to another (the licensee) of this right to use the licensed rights free of suit by the property owner, pursuant to certain terms and conditions and subject to certain limitations.

The extent of the rights granted in a license may run the gamut from a mere permission to use the licensed property in some limited manner (a nonexclusive license) to all but ownership of the property (an exclusive license). (For more on this topic, see Chapter 2.)

Interesting Facts

- In the United States, royalties from patent licensing have increased from $15 billion in 1990 to more than $110 billion in 2000.

- Licensing experts believe that a well-managed IP portfolio should yield 1 percent of a firm's revenues and 5 percent of its net profits. At the same time, however, a recent survey found that two-thirds of U.S. companies own IP that is neither used internally nor licensed to others.

- Investors value a dollar of royalty income four to five times as highly as a dollar of operating earnings.

- Intellectual property was deemed an important factor driving mergers and acquisitions by 51 percent of surveyed business executives.

Clearly, there is money to be made from licensing intellectual property (and from writing books about licensing IP). More significantly, the practice of such licensing is now so widespread and accepted as to be expected by market analysts, shareholders, directors—and those who decide on executives' salaries and bonuses. Indeed, today it is the failure to license which is deemed noteworthy—and unacceptable.

Why, Tell Me Why!

Why license your (or your firm's) intellectual property? There are several reasons. The most commonly heard, and still the most significant, is *money*. Licensing creates revenue. Most licenses bear royalties, either in the form of a lump sum (a paid-up license) or periodic payments based on sales (a running royalty license). Some licenses bear no royalties but are, in effect, an exchange of rights between two IP owners (a cross license). If, however, you consider the cost savings realized by securing a license under the property of another without payment of a cash royalty, even a cross license may be deemed to generate an imputed income.

Beyond the mere generation of royalty income (by itself, no mean accomplishment), licensing may be utilized as a vehicle for entry into new geographic or product markets. A property owner may grant a license allowing a licensee entry into a geographic market not served by the licensor or allowing introduction of a product not offered by the licensor. The licensee bears all of the risks attendant on such a new venture and pays a royalty for the privilege. The licensor collects the royalty and observes the licensee. If the licensee's efforts prove successful, the licensor may enter the market as well (assuming, of course, that the license was not exclusive; more on this later). If, however, the licensee's efforts end in failure, the licensor has learned a valuable lesson at no cost to itself.

Somewhat ironically, licensing may, under some circumstances, also serve to strengthen the licensor's market position. Many firms will refuse to purchase a product available only from a single source, thereby placing themselves somewhat at the supplier's mercy. Such firms will demand that a patentee, for example, grant licenses to others (automobile manufacturers are famous—or infamous—for this).

Licensees also may serve to provide variety and breadth of choice in a market where a monopolist is able to offer only a limited product line. Similarly, they may develop improvements or ancillary products or services, all of which serve to increase the attractiveness of the basic, licensed product. A moderate slice of a large pie may well be bigger than all of a small pie.

Licensing also has the effect of strengthening the licensed properties. In part, this is the result of co-opting of potential infringers (i.e., converting them into licensees). With respect to patents, a further benefit obtains. The recognition, by others, of the validity of patent rights, as evidenced by the presence of licensees paying royalties ("putting their money where their mouth is"), is deemed by the courts to be a "secondary indicia of patentability" (a good thing!). The more licenses that are granted, the stronger the licensed patents become (the greater the likelihood the validity of the patent will be upheld at trial).

By broadening the availability of a patented technology, licensing may lead to the incorporation of the technology into an industry standard. The implications of such incorporation on future royalty income should be readily apparent to all. Finally, licensing of a pioneering invention or technology may reduce the concerns of those charged with enforcement of the antitrust laws (or reduce the threat of those who might seek to utilize these laws for their own purposes).

What to License

Having seen all the benefits to be derived from licensing, the reader is probably asking, "How can I get in on this great opportunity?" After some thought, it seems that the proper question is really "Which of my intellectual properties should I seek to license?" (If you don't have any intellectual property, you've got a bit of a problem.)

The starting point, obviously, is a thorough analysis of the intellectual property portfolio, the contents of which can be broadly divided into two categories: property that is in use and property that is not in use. It is commonly believed that any property not in use is available to be licensed. Not necessarily so. Some unused IP is held and maintained specifically to deny it to a competitor or potential competitor. Check before you start offering such unused property to any and all comers. Some property is unused because it is simply unworkable, obsolete, or otherwise not commercially desirable. Check before investing substantial efforts in licensing a property. If a patented technology is unused and not likely to be used in the future, is not to be denied to others, and is not attracting any licensees, you should abandon it and save any future prosecution costs or maintenance fees.

Properties that are in use are divided, by some commentators (a euphemism for prolific writers with little experience), into those used in key products or services (so-called core properties) and those used only in ancillary or less important products or services or not at all (not surprisingly, known as noncore properties). At least until relatively recently, it was conventional wisdom that noncore properties may be licensed, but core properties—the "crown jewels"—are to be held inviolate. With respect to the noncore properties, the conventional wisdom is correct. With respect to the core properties, it is *wrong*. As noted, the market for a product or service—even a key product or service—may, under some circumstances, actually increase as the result of licensing an underlying technology. Moreover, there may well be market segments that the property owner cannot address, does not wish to address, or cannot fully satisfy. Such market segments offer licensing opportunities. The conclusion to be drawn is simply this: Any useful properties should be considered as licensing candidates, while any nonuseful properties should be considered as candidates for abandonment.

The Extent of Licensing in the U.S. Economy

A Bedtime Story

Once upon a time, a long time ago, there lived several domestic commercial tribes of people. Each of these tribes owned trees that gave forth fruits, from which they made various products upon which they feasted. The managers of these tribes built great legal castles where they hid their trees to protect them from dragons and ogres and others that might wish to eat the fruit. As time went by, however, many of the trees suffered from lack of cross-pollination due to their isolation and produced less and less fruit. Some of the trees expired, either having reached the end of their statutory terms or from other causes, and were not replaced. Steadily, the fruit harvest diminished. At the same time, unnoticed by the managers, a portion of the fruits, of a variety not used by the tribes, were left hanging on the branches of the trees until they rotted and fell away. Ultimately, many of the tribes began to go hungry and their numbers became fewer and fewer.

As they cast about for a means to assuage their hunger, the managers noticed that one tribe—in Texas—continued to feast regularly and, indeed, grew large and prospered. And so it came to pass that the managers from the other tribes studied the ways of the wise and successful Texan managers. They observed that the Texans did not hide their trees in the dark. Indeed, they allowed others to pick from their trees those fruits that the Texans themselves did not use—and sometimes the Texans even shared with others the fruits they *did* use. The others paid the Texans great royalties for the fruits they took. The managers who observed this predicted that the Texans' trees would soon be exhausted and their harvest would diminish; but, to their wonderment, the Texan's trees blossomed. The managers also saw the Texans exchange fruits with other tribes and use the new fruits they obtained to make new products.

Some of the managers refused to change from their old ways. They're now flipping burgers for the McDonald tribe. Other, more enlightened, managers adapted the practices of the Texans and lived happily ever after.

THE END

Summary

A license is a grant by an intellectual property owner to another party (the licensee) of the rights to use the IP. A license may be royalty-bearing or non–royalty-bearing (as in cross licenses), and a royalty-bearing license may be either paid-up or bear a running royalty, where the royalty is based on the sales of the licensed goods or services.

CHAPTER 2

Basic Contract Law

After reading this chapter you will be able to

- Understand the basic elements of a contract and, more specifically, of a license

- Understand the advantages conferred by a written, as opposed to an oral agreement

- Know how to ensure that you are contracting with the right party

- Identify the requirements for a valid contract

- Ensure that a license is enforceable

Elements of a Contract

Promises, Promises

Having defined "license" (if you've forgotten already, see Chapter 1), we now inform the reader that a license is a form of contract. Without delving too deeply into the mystical realm of the "legal fraternity," it can be said that a contract is simply a promise that is legally enforceable. As with any promise, a contract can be "express" (explicitly stated) or "implied" (created by actions or circumstances). An express contract may be set forth in a written document (whereupon it is termed a "written contract" by the clever lawyers). If it is not "reduced to writing" (lawyerspeak meaning that someone—preferably a highly paid attorney—wrote it down some-where), it is called an "oral" or "verbal" contract. It is thought by some (known in the legal profession as fools) that only written contracts are enforceable. Not necessarily so. Although some contracts—notably including those for the sale of land, for the sale of goods valued in excess of $500, or that cannot be totally performed within a year—must be written if they are to be enforceable, licenses are generally not among them. An oral license may well be enforceable. This is not to say, how-ever, that a written contract is not preferable to an oral one. Indeed, written contracts offer several advantages, not the least of which is that their terms are definite, immutable, and permanent.

Many times contracting parties, after discussing the terms of a contract for some time, will conclude that they have reached agreement. Often, however, the understanding of the two parties is not at all the same. Putting the agreement on paper forces both parties to look at it, thereby uncovering any differences in their understanding of what has been agreed.

Memories are fallible (not surprisingly, this is especially so when money is at stake) and grow dim after time. Years from now, will the parties clearly and correctly remember the agreement they reached today? How much better to be able to refer to a written record, should the need arise.

Even if memories were perfect, people die, move, or otherwise become unavailable, often at the most inconvenient time. An oral con-tract may die or disappear with them. A written record may be all that prevents a decedent from taking a contract to the grave.

Earth, Air, Fire, and Water

Despite what some lawyers would have you believe, contracts are not all that complicated. There are only four (4)* critical elements of a contract (see Exhibit 2.1):

---

*When referring to a number, lawyers typically present it in words, followed by the corre-sponding numerals in parentheses. This is considered an element of style in legal writing.

1. Offer and acceptance

2. Competent parties

3. Consideration

4. Legal purpose

Offer and Acceptance. A contract is formed when the parties reach an agreement to which they mutually assent. Most often one party proposes a bargain (the offer) and the other party agrees to the proposal (the acceptance). The test for the existence of an agreement is an objective one. It matters not what you thought. If a "reasonable person" (modern version of the old "reasonable man" rule) in the position of the other party would have concluded from your acts or words that agreement had been reached, a contract has been formed. Where the subject matter of the proposed transaction is a business one, it usually will be presumed (by the court) that the parties intended that their agreement be legally binding. All of this means, of course, that contract negotiations, like auctions, are no place to kid around. Don't say anything you are not willing to be bound to do.

EXHIBIT 2.1

Elements of a Contract

Offer and Acceptance between Competent Parties

+ Consideration + Legal Purpose

= CONTRACT

Sometimes an offer and acceptance are not sufficient to create a legally enforceable contract. No contract is formed if the agreement of the parties is too indefinite. Such agreements are termed "fatally indefinite." In order to be legally enforceable (as opposed to enforceable by large gentlemen in ill-fitting suits), an agreement must include all of the *necessary* terms. To no one's surprise, it is often difficult to determine which terms may be necessary. The test is whether the court can (1) determine whether one party has breached the agreement and (2) has a reasonably certain basis for awarding a remedy. Omitted terms, which are not *necessary*, will be supplied by the court on a "reasonable" basis. If you don't want some stranger deciding the terms of your contract, make sure you decide them yourself. For a checklist of most conceivable license terms, see Appendix A.

Occasionally negotiating parties recognize the need for a term but are unable to reach agreement. They solve this dilemma by formally agreeing to reach agreement, with regard to this term, at some time in the future. This practice, which for some reason is more widespread overseas than in the United States, is known as agreeing to agree. *Do not do this.* If you can't agree now, why do you expect to be able to agree later—when the issue may be even more contentious? Traditionally (euphemism for "in the old days when people still respected lawyers"), failure to reach agreement as to the missing term left an agreement *fatally indefinite.* The modern view (euphemism for "at a time when lawyers are suing McDonald's for selling fattening food") is that the missing term may be supplied by the court.

Finally, if the parties achieve a mutual assent as to all necessary terms of an agreement and decide to memorialize that agreement in writing, is the writing a necessary prerequisite to a legally enforceable contract? What happens if the written agreement is not produced or not executed by both parties? Generally the courts follow the intent of the parties. If the parties' manifest intention was to be bound even before a legal document was prepared, the court will find an enforceable contract although the document is never prepared. Similarly, if the parties' intent was not to be bound until a document has been prepared and duly executed, the court will not find an enforceable contract. Where the parties have not expressed an intent, the court will likely find that an enforceable contract was formed when assent was reached.

Party Time. If a contract is to be enforceable, the parties thereto must be "competent." Parties who are "infants" or "mentally infirm" may avoid (lawyerspeak for "get out of") their contracts. "Infants" are minors,— now generally defined by law as individuals under the age of 18. The "mentally infirm" include the insane, the senile, and the mentally retarded. (Bear this in mind before calling a party with whom you are negotiating a "moron.") Intoxication also is legally deemed to be an infirmity. Therefore, serve the drinks *after* the contract has been signed. Indeed, if a party is both slightly drunk and slightly infirm, and the courts determine that advantage has been taken of that party's infirmity, the infirm party may be allowed to avoid the contract.

Not only must you assure that the party with whom you are negotiating is competent (admittedly, this is sometimes a close question), you also must verify that you are, in fact, contracting with the proper party. A putative licensor (Note: Use of the word "putative" will impress people at cocktail parties, especially those who have had a few drinks.) may not actually own the properties you seek to license. Check it. Publicly available records of the United States Patent and Trademark Office (USPTO) can be examined to determine the current ownership of U.S. patents and federally registered trademarks. This examination can now be done online. After investigating the matter and/or receiving oral assurances (for whatever value those may have), get a written representation. (When in doubt, get it in writing; when not in doubt, get it in writing anyway.) Specifically, a licensor should provide a written representation (see the end of this chapter for a definition of "representation") that it, he, she or they, as the case may be, owns the properties being licensed.

Similarly, seek assurance that there is no bar or impediment to the grant of the proposed license. If, for example, the subject intellectual property has previously been licensed to another on an exclusive basis, the property owner can no longer effectively grant a license to you. If you are seeking a sublicense, verify that the grant of such sublicense is permitted by the license from the property owner.

The Organization Man. Organizations act through their duly authorized agents. When dealing with an organization, make sure that such a representative executes the agreement ("executes" means "signs" but sounds a lot more impressive) in a representative capacity. The signature of the representative, without a title and affiliation, may merely bind the individual, not the organization. Proper execution on behalf of an organization should include the name of the organization and the title of the representative. The title of the individual should be such as to lead one to reasonably believe that the individual actually has the authority to bind the organization to the agreement. The president of a corporation almost certainly has authority to commit the corporation to a license. The receptionist almost certainly does not.

Consider This. With a few esoteric exceptions, none of which apply to licensing, all contracts must be "supported by consideration." "Consideration," in simple terms, is what you are giving for what you are getting. Most often consideration takes the form of an exchange of promises between the contracting parties. In the context of a license, the licensor promises to allow (and perhaps enable) the licensee to utilize some rights under certain intellectual property; and the licensee promises to pay a royalty to the licensor (or, perhaps, cross license the rights).

It is said by some (some lawyers, that is) that a contract may fail for lack of consideration. In a theoretical sense, this is true. In a practical sense, however, the courts will not inquire into the adequacy of consideration, and the consideration provided by the two parties to a license need not be roughly equivalent. It will suffice that the consideration provided by each is not nonexistent. Therefore, consider carefully (pun intended) and do not expect the courts to save you from a bad deal.

Legal Purpose. The last requirement for an enforceable contract is that its purpose not be one that is unlawful or contrary to public policy. The list of such disapproved purposes is, fortunately, quite short. The courts in most states will not enforce contracts for the payment of gambling debts. Nor will they enforce contracts for the sale of controlled substances or employment contracts for hit men (although, as a practical matter, court enforcement of such employment contracts may be unnecessary). The only concerns as to illegal purpose, which may arise in the context of a license, relate to the antitrust laws and laws regulating franchising (see Chapter 7). If you feel you absolutely must violate these laws, do not expect the courts to enforce those provisions of your license creating the violation.

The law is a living thing and, like all living things, sometimes is unpredictable. What if the law changes after a contract is executed, such that the contract, which was previously acceptable, is now unlawful? In such cases, both parties are discharged, and the court awards restitution to return the parties as near as possible to the positions they occupied prior to contracting (the *status quo ante*, for all you lovers of Latin).

A Clear Conscience

As a practical matter, few contracts are found unenforceable due to an illegal purpose. A related and more common problem, however, arises with respect to the doctrine of "unconscionability." If the provisions of a contract are so grossly unfair as to shock the conscience of the court, the court may refuse to enforce the contract, or may refuse to enforce any unconscionable provision, or may so limit the application of any unconscionable provision as to avoid any unconscionable result. This last option is known as contract reformation. Unconscionability may be either "procedural" or "substantive." *Procedural unconscionability* occurs when one party is induced to enter a contract without having a meaningful choice. Such contracts, when no bargaining is possible, are known as contracts of adhesion. Typically they involve high-pressure salespeople misleading illiterate consumers. Contracts of adhesion also may be found where the parties are of vastly different economic power.

Substantive unconscionability results when contract provisions are truly unfair and one-sided. Generally, substantive unconscionability is found where prices are excessive or the remedies of one of the parties have been modified in an unfair manner. Most often such unfair modifications involve unreasonably large, liquidated damages ("liquidated damages" are a predetermined penalty for a breach of contract) or, in the case of a contract involving consumer goods, a limitation of consequential damages for any personal injury that may occur. (Such limitation is deemed to be contrary to public policy.)

Fair Means or Foul?

Although not, strictly speaking, a contract element, each contract includes an implicit covenant (lawyerspeak for "promise") of good faith and fair dealing. This requirement, quite literally, covers a multitude of sins; if you commit a sin, you've breached the covenant. There is no clear definition of "unfairness." It is akin to pornography, of which a Supreme Court justice once said (after much study of the subject), "I can't define it, but I know it when I see it."

General Structure of a License

Introductions—The Preamble

Most contracts, and hence most licenses, follow a roughly similar format, which starts with the identification of the contracting parties (see Exhibit 2.2). If either or both of the parties is a "juristic person" (an organization such as a corporation or limited liability company), it is common to identify the state in which it was organized (. . . a corporation of the State of. . .). If such party has its principal place of business in a state other than the one in which it was created, this fact may also be recited (. . . having a principal place of business at. . .). Contrary to popular belief, these recitations are not mere padding intended to justify lawyers' fees (although they do that). They provide support for claims to legal jurisdiction over the organization, by the courts of the states so identified, in the event litigation should ensue.

Following the introductions, there generally appear a number of clauses (not sentences—it is a stylistic requirement that all but the last clause end in a semicolon, not a period) beginning with the word "WHEREAS" (the truly style-conscious capitalize the entire word). These clauses are not present merely to fill space. They (it is hoped) state facts leading to the formation of the contract as well as the intentions or goals of the parties. In the event of an ambiguity, the court may utilize them in defining the parties' intent. If a court is called on to supply an omitted contract term, it will search these clauses for guidance. (Alternatively, it may toss a coin, read tea leaves, or examine entrails.) Finally, these clauses may be considered when questions of unconscionability are raised.

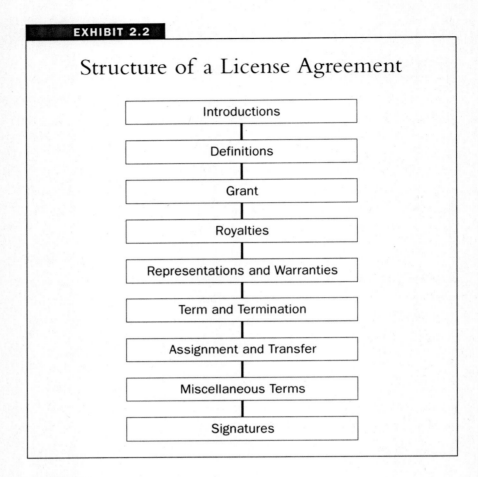

EXHIBIT 2.2

Structure of a License Agreement

- Introductions
- Definitions
- Grant
- Royalties
- Representations and Warranties
- Term and Termination
- Assignment and Transfer
- Miscellaneous Terms
- Signatures

Definitions

It has been said that, in legal disputes, whoever defines the terms wins the argument. It also has been said that undefined terms put lawyers' children through college. When "memorializing an agreement" (another lawyerspeak term meaning "writing it down on paper"), be sure to define all of the terms that are used in the agreement. When presented with a draft of an agreement prepared by another, carefully study the definitions. Make sure they reflect the intentions of the parties (or, at least, *your* intentions).

Definitions may be "inclusive," specifying that which is included within the defined term, or "exclusive," specifying that which is not included. Similarly, definitions may be "open," allowing for the inclusion of further, unstated items or terms, or "closed," limited only to that which has been stated. Two definitions that look quite similar can have very different impacts on an agreement.

After examining the definitions set forth in a contract, note how they are used in the contract text. A good (advantageous) definition can be undone by the manner in which it is used. Beware of double negatives—a favorite tool (euphemism for "trick") of attorneys.

Grant—Like Ulysses, It's General

In essence, the "grant" is the heart of a license. It is here that the licensor actually bestows on the licensee the right to use the licensed properties, and it is here that the scope and nature of this permission are specified.

In the grant, the licensed rights or properties are identified and any limits on the extent or manner of their use are specified, as are the geographical and temporal bounds of the license. While the grant is the heart of the license, it may, like the heart of a bank loan officer, be small and hard to find. This is primarily because it relies on the use of words or phrases, the meanings of which are set forth in the definitions.

In addition to defining the scope of the license, the grant may specify the ability (or inability) of the licensor to grant further licenses and, similarly, the ability (or inability) of the licensee to transfer or "assign" the license to a third party or to grant "sublicenses."

A license may be "exclusive" or "nonexclusive." A nonexclusive license is a mere covenant not to sue. So long as the nonexclusive licensee complies with all of the terms and conditions of the license agreement, the licensor will forbear to sue. The licensor remains free, however, to itself use the licensed rights and to grant additional licenses to others. A nonexclusive licensee should not, therefore, expect to obtain—or to maintain—a monopoly with respect to the licensed rights. An exclusive license divests the licensor of the right to grant further licenses of the exclusively licensed rights. It also deprives the licensor of the right to itself utilize the licensed properties. A hybrid form of license, not commonly seen, is essentially exclusive but allows the licensor to utilize the properties also. Such a license is known in Canada and the United Kingdom as a sole license. (For more on this topic, see Chapter 4.)

A license may be "assignable" or "nonassignable." An "assignable" license is one that may be transferred, or assigned by the licensee to a third party, which then replaces the original licensee. A "nonassignable" license is (duh!) one that may not be assigned. In practice, many licenses are neither assignable without any restriction nor absolutely nonassignable. Rather, they can be assigned under certain narrowly specified conditions. In such cases, the grant may simply state the more appropriate of the two basic options ("assignable" and "nonassignable"), and the specific terms and conditions relating to assignment are set forth in a separate section of the agreement, usually creatively entitled "Assignment." Generally, licenses where the royalties are paid in a lump sum at the inception of the license ("paid-up" licenses) should be nonassignable.

It is extremely frustrating (and possibly damaging to a career) to grant a paid-up license to a small firm, at a correspondingly small royalty, only to see the licensee transfer the license to a much larger firm that makes much more extensive use of the licensed rights but pays nothing. This problem can be avoided, of course, by insisting on a license where the royalty is determined by the amount of sales of licensed products ("running royalty" licenses). A running royalty, however, may be uneconomical for the licensor to administer or unduly burdensome on the licensee. The licensee may, moreover, insist on the right to assign the license in the event that it becomes involved in a merger or acquisition. Therefore, when granting a paid-up license to any but the largest firms, limit use by any assignee to the level of use of the assignor immediately preceding the assignment.

 TIPS & TECHNIQUES

Under most circumstances, a paid-up license should limit the usage rights a licensee can grant to an assignee to the licensee's level of use immediately prior to the assignment.

Assignment of a running royalty license is, again generally, not a significant problem. Any firm willing to pay royalties at the established rate is welcome aboard. The major caveat here is with regard to those firms that are known to be dishonest, unreliable, or financially unsound: A licensor would not appreciate finding such a firm as the assignee of one of his or her licenses. To prevent this, assignment—when allowed—is made "subject to the approval of the licensor, which shall not be unreasonably withheld."

Finally, it is to be noted that the matter of assignment is not always within the control of the licensor. Sometimes, as when a licensee becomes bankrupt, it is subject to the laws of bankruptcy. In order to avoid putting a license into the hands of an unknown bankruptcy trustee, it is common to provide that a license will automatically terminate if the licensee becomes illiquid or otherwise exhibits conditions suggesting that bankruptcy is imminent.

Royalties—The Price to Be Paid

After detailing what the licensor is giving to the licensee—that is, the grant—it is common for a license agreement to specify what the licensee is giving to the licensor—that is, the royalties. Royalties are discussed in some detail in Chapter 9.

Representations and Warranties—
What Is and What Will Be

"Representations" (called "reps" by certain pathetic individuals who think this makes them sound cool) are statements as to the current state of affairs. Such statements are intended to be relied on as the basis for the agreement between the parties. When a representation proves to be untrue (euphemism for "a damned lie"), it is known as a "misrepresentation" and, if "material," that is, of sufficient significance, provides a basis for termination of the contract by the party to which it was addressed.

While a representation speaks of the present, a warranty speaks to the future. A "warranty" is a promise, by one party, that certain statements are true and will remain so. If the promise is broken, the party to which it was made may recover any resultant damages.

Often, when a written contract becomes the subject of litigation, evidence of any oral statements or promises, made by one party and relied on by the other, are excluded. (This is known as the parole evidence rule and has nothing to do with getting out of jail.) Thus, it is important that such statements—the representations and warranties—be set forth in writing. In simple terms, if you intend to rely on it, get it in writing.

TIPS & TECHNIQUES

If you intend to rely on anything, get it in writing.

Term and Termination—As Time Goes By

Other than taxes and telemarketer phone calls, nothing goes on forever. A contract, unless breached or terminated by agreement of the parties, goes on until it reaches the end of its "term." The term of a contract may be a fixed period, with or without "extensions" or "renewals," or until the occurrence of some future event.

A license does not simply end; it "terminates." The parties do not simply shake hands and walk away; they wrap up matters in accordance with predetermined "termination" provisions. Such provisions typically pertain to disposal of inventories and work in progress, fulfillment of existing contracts and warranty obligations, return of confidential documents and proprietary tools and jigs, and payment of accrued royalties and royalties accruing during termination.

Assignment and Transfer—
The Third Man Theme

A license, like a marriage, is a close, personal relationship. Most married people would be shocked to wake up one morning to find a stranger beside them in bed. Society generally frowns on this sort of behavior in the context of a marriage, but, unless restricted or prohibited by the license terms, it is allowed by law in the context of a license. So, unless you thrill to the excitement of relations with strangers, consider the appropriate limitations to be placed on assignment of rights and duties under a license or on the substitution of a new party for the one with which you had originally contracted.

As a practical matter, once a license has been executed, the role of the licensor is largely, if not totally, passive. It is the licensee that is utilizing the licensed property and is responsible for the continued payment of any running royalties. It is the licensee that is responsible for the proper marking of patent numbers, the maintenance of quality standards of goods sold under licensed trademarks, and the maintenance of confidentiality of licensed trade secrets. An unreliable licensee may fail in its business, causing a loss of royalty income. More important, an unreliable licensee may cause irreparable harm by failing to mark (more on this later—see Chapter 5), lowering quality and disclosing confidential information. You carefully chose (or you should have) the party that became your licensee. Don't allow a stranger to take that party's place.

Miscellaneous Terms— Lost in the Maddening Crowd

At the end of a contract, there generally appear a number of relatively standardized provisions derided by all and sundry as "boilerplate." Many people stop reading when they reach this point (of the contract; not, it is hoped, of this book), assuming that the remainder is of no real consequence. *Do not do this.* Among the terms that may, or may not, be found here are most favored nations clauses, choice of laws provisions, arbitration provisions, and "nonwaiver" clauses.

A "most favored nations" clause is a requirement that the terms and conditions of the license are at least as favorable (to the licensee) as those previously *or thereafter* granted to any other licensee. If, in the future, more favorable terms are granted to another, such terms also must be offered to the licensee. In some cases, the more advantageous terms must be made retroactive. The existence of such a provision may seriously limit the licensor's flexibility in negotiating with potential licensees in the future and should, therefore, not be accepted lightly—or through inattention—as it often comprises an invitation to future litigation.

Most contracts include a statement that it is to be "construed," "interpreted," "governed," or whatever in accord with the laws of a specified state. Laymen (political correctness notwithstanding, "laywomen" sounds gross) often believe that such a selection means that any ensuing litigation of the contract will be in the specified state. *Wrong.* Such a provision merely means that the court which hears the case may be required to apply the laws of a "foreign" state ("foreign" means "other than itself"). Jurisdiction (the ability of courts to hear a case) is conferred only by a statement specifically referring to it. On occasion, parties in different states choose a "neutral" third state as the forum for any disputes. *Do not do this.* The parties cannot confer jurisdiction on the courts of a state that has no relation to the parties or their dispute. Such an election is effective only to demonstrate the ignorance of the parties.

In an effort to facilitate the (relatively) prompt and (comparatively) inexpensive resolution of any disputes that may arise, the parties may agree to submit such disputes to binding arbitration. Such a provision will be honored, even encouraged, by the courts. It is nevertheless necessary to specify which disputes are to be arbitrated—all disputes arising out of the license or only certain ones. If less than all disputes are identified in the arbitration provision, litigation as to those disputes not specifically referred to arbitration remains a possibility. Unlike choosing a court jurisdiction, the parties are free to choose any locale and rules for their arbitration.

There are times when a party to an agreement may choose not to enforce a provision or may simply overlook a breach or failure to perform by the other party. Such forbearance or inattention may give rise to a "waiver," that is, an inability to enforce that provision in the future. To prevent such a result, the parties (or one of them, if the other isn't looking) may include a provision stating that no waiver will arise. Such a provision is neutral, favoring neither party. However, before relying on the other party's inactivity as establishing a precedent, check to see if your contract includes a nonwaiver provision.

Summary

A license is a form of contract. Although enforceable contracts may be either oral or written, using a written contract offers many significant advantages. There are four critical elements of a contract: offer and acceptance, competent parties, consideration, and legal purpose. Mere offer and acceptance are not enough to form a legally binding contract if the agreement is too indefinite ("fatally indefinite"). Negotiating parties should thus be sure to include all the necessary terms. If a written contract was never prepared, the courts will follow the intent of the parties: If their intent was to be bound before the document was prepared, the agreement is binding; if their intent was to be bound only after the preparation and execution of a written agreement, the agreement is not binding.

The party licensing the intellectual property must actually own it and thus have the right to license it. The persons executing the license on behalf of each party must have the authority to commit their respective parties to a license.

Generally, a contract begins with the identification of the contracting parties, followed by a number of clauses that state facts about the reason for the formation of the contract as well as the intentions and goals of the contracting parties. Next, the terms used in the agreement are defined. Following the definitions is the grant, which identifies the licensed rights or properties and details the limits on their use. Next are representations, which are statements as to the current state of affairs, and warranties, which are promises, by one party, that certain statements are true and will remain so. "Termination provisions" detail the responsibilities of each party at the end (termination) of the license. Finally, "miscellaneous terms" may include most favored nations clauses, choice of laws provisions, arbitration provisions, and nonwaiver clauses.

CHAPTER 3

Intellectual Property Primer

After reading this chapter you will be able to

- Understand the various types of patents
- Recognize the components of a utility patent
- Identify the advantages a provisional patent application bestows upon the filer
- Understand how copyrights, patents, trademarks, and other forms of IP differ
- Understand why semiconductor chips aren't protectable by patents or copyrights
- Review the types of agreements an employer can use to keep the company's employees from depleting the company's intellectual capital

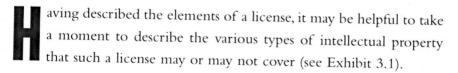aving described the elements of a license, it may be helpful to take a moment to describe the various types of intellectual property that such a license may or may not cover (see Exhibit 3.1).

Patents

A patent conveys to its owner the right to prevent others from making, using, selling, offering for sale (this is a recent addition), or importing the patented invention. Patents are national in nature, having effect only within the territory of the issuing country.

EXHIBIT 3.1

IP Protection

	Utility Patent	Design Patent	Trademark/ Service Mark	Copyright	Trade Secret	Mask Work	Registered Design
Protects	Products, devices, processes, computer programs, business methods	Industrial design, web page design	Words, phrases, symbols, or colors that identify the source of goods or service	Expressions of creative works, such as pictures, novels, music performance, advertising copy, computer source code, etc.	Confidential information that is maintained secret	Mask works— stencils used for semiconductor chip manufacturing	Industrial designs, web page design
Term (in years)	20	14	Perpetual, so long as used	70 minimum	Perpetual, as long as secret is maintained	10	10
Registration required	Yes	Yes	No	No	No	Yes	Yes
Examined	Yes	Yes	Yes	No	N/A	No	No
Cost to Obtain and Maintain	High	Medium	Low	Low	Low	Low	Low

The patent law of the United States provides for three kinds of patents:

1. Plant patents

2. Design patents

3. Utility patents

Plant patents cover asexually reproduced plants and are primarily of interest only to plant breeders. Design patents cover the ornamental design of an article (its appearance) to the extent that the design or appearance is dictated by aesthetic, rather than functional, considerations. The majority of patents are of the third kind—utility patents—and it is with these that we shall be mostly, but not exclusively, concerned.

A utility patent, generally speaking, may cover a device or an article, a composition of matter, a method or a process of doing or making something, or, less commonly, a new application for an existing device or material or an old or known product made by a particular new process.

Formerly, a U.S. utility patent had a term of 17 years, commencing on the patent's issue date. Under current law, however, utility patents have a term of 20 years, commencing on the date of filing of the application on which it is based. The new law applies to patents issuing on applications filed on or after June 8, 1995. Patents issued on earlier-filed applications now have a term of either 17 years from the date of issue or 20 years from the date of filing, whichever is longer. Although in theory the term of a utility patent may be extended if its prosecution is unduly delayed by the Patent Office, as a practical matter, the patent term is nonextendable. The primary exception is for patents directed to pharmaceutical products, in which case the term may be extended to compensate for time lost in securing the applicable regulatory (Food and Drug Administration [FDA]) approval. Design patents have a term of 14 years from the date of issue.

As a result of statutory requirements and rules promulgated by the United States Patent and Trademark Office (USPTO), the format and content of utility patents is relatively standardized. Preceding the textual portions of the patent are one or more pages of drawings of the "preferred embodiment" of the invention. The patent text begins with a brief statement identifying the subject of the invention. A background section, which states the problem that is solved by the invention, follows this section. This statement of the problem may include a description of prior solutions or attempted solutions and the reasons why they were not wholly satisfactory. Following the background section is a section summarizing the invention, including its key features and advantages. Next is a section providing a brief description of the patent drawings, specifying what is being illustrated in each figure. After this is a rather lengthy section setting forth a detailed description of the invention with reference to the "preferred embodiment" illustrated in the drawings. These textual portions of the utility patent are known as the specification. The patent concludes with the patent claims, which are the consecutively numbered sentences at the end of the patent document. Preceding the patent drawings is a cover sheet, which includes a brief abstract, a representative drawing, and a wealth of other useful information.

Understanding Patent Claims—Rules of the Road

As it is the claims of a patent that determine its scope, an understanding of the basic tenets of claim construction is exceedingly important. Patent claims are composed of limitations—phrases that identify and describe, or limit, the various components (or steps, in the case of a method or process claim) of the claimed invention. The various words and phrases that appear in the patent claims are to be interpreted or construed according to their normal or accustomed meaning. If no such accepted definition exists—that is, if the patent draftsperson has created or coined new words or phrases, or has used words or phrases in an unconventional manner (according to an old and often quoted decision, each patent drafter is his or her own lexicographer)—the patent specification is used as a guide to claim interpretation. If no clear definition is provided in the patent specification, the record of the prosecution of the patent application (known as the file wrapper and available from the Patent Office) is examined. As a last resort (and only then), standard reference materials—extrinsic sources—are considered.

Every word in a patent claim is deemed to have meaning and significance. None may be ignored. Substantive patent law prohibits two patent claims from covering exactly the same invention. Thus, if (as often happens) two patent claims are largely identical, the nonidentical portions *must* be so construed as to have different meanings. (This is known as the *doctrine of claim differentiation.*)

Claim terms may not be construed in a manner inconsistent with arguments or statements made by the applicant during prosecution of the patent application, nor contrary to reasons that may have been enunciated by the patent examiner as the basis for claim allowance (the *doctrine of file wrapper estoppel*).

Claims—actually constituent claim limitations—must be construed so as to preserve patentability. In the event that a pertinent new (not considered during the prosecution of the patent application) prior art reference is discovered, the patent claims must be interpreted, if at all possible, so as to distinguish the new invention from the prior art reference and, hence, to maintain the validity of the claims. Also, if at all possible, claims should be construed so as to cover the embodiment(s) of the inventions described in the patent specification.

If these rules seem complex and confusing, they are! As evidenced by the number of reversals handed down by the Court of Appeals for the Federal Circuit (the CAFC, the patent appeals court), many trial judges of the federal district courts get it wrong themselves.

Independent Claims, Dependent Claims—
A Way to Simplify the Task of Claim Construction

Patent claims are of two kinds: independent claims and dependent claims. *Independent claims* are those that do not refer to another, preceding claim. Hence, the first claim of a patent (claim 1) is always independent (there are no preceding claims). *Dependent claims* incorporate by reference each and every limitation of each of the claims from which they depend (i.e., to which they refer). Many patents include long chains or series of dependent claims, each referring to—and incorporating the limitations of—a preceding claim. Each dependent claim is narrower (i.e., more limited in scope) than the claim from which it depends. Thus, if an independent claim is not infringed, no claim that depends from it (and therefore is of more limited scope) can be infringed. For this reason, attention is inevitably focused on the independent claims, which are generally much fewer in number. In most instances, the dependent claims may be safely ignored.

Provisional Patent Rights—Life before Birth

Among the many popular misconceptions concerning patents, one of the most enduring is that patents have effect as of the date of filing. A surprising number of people believed (and continue to believe) that a patent springs to life, fully formed, upon filing. Such people occasionally wander into attorneys' offices, clutching a copy of a newly filed patent application—more often than not, an application they filed themselves—to seek enforcement of their patent against one or more alleged infringers. Such enforcement is impossible, however, because patents have effect only from the date of issue. Moreover, until recently, patents had no retroactive effect. No liability for patent infringement could arise from any activities occurring prior the date of patent issue. However, to an extent—and *only* to an extent—this nonretroactivity of patent protection has been altered by recent changes in the patent law, which have created provisional patent rights. These same changes also have reversed the prior rule that pending patent applications be maintained in secret, by the Patent Office, until the patent is issued.

Under the new law, patent applications filed on or after November 29, 2000, are published 18 months after their filing date (actually, 18 months after the earliest claimed filing date; discuss this with a patent practitioner). When an application is published, the entire file wrapper is open to inspection and copying by the public. Moreover, members of the public may, within two months of publication, submit prior art documents to the Patent Office to be considered by the patent examiner during examination of the application.

Once a patent application has been published and an accused infringer has been given actual notice thereof, certain provisional rights apply. If the published patent application ultimately matures into an issued patent, having claims substantially similar (although as yet undecided by the courts, the term "substantially similar" probably means "virtually identical") to those previously published, the patentee—upon issue of the patent—may recover, in addition to other damages, a reasonable royalty in respect of infringement of those claims that occurred during the period between the publication of the application and the issue of the patent. Thus, a certain measure of retroactivity has been introduced into the patent system.

Trade Secrets and Know-how

A *trade secret* is information that is not generally available and that confers a competitive advantage on its possessor. It may, for example, comprise a chemical formula, a manufacturing process, a machine design, or a business method. Note that the secret need not be absolute; it is necessary only that the information in question is not widely known.

However, general knowledge cannot be converted into a trade secret simply by labeling it as such.

Know-how is similar to trade secrets. Essentially, it comprises a body of information, the components of which may be individually known, but the compilation of which has competitive value. Supplier lists, parts specifications, and quality assurance and testing procedures generally fall into this category.

Although there are no formalities associated with trade secrets, it is necessary that the subject information be treated as a secret. This requirement is often overlooked. If information is to be accorded trade secret status, it must be treated as a secret by its possessor. At a minimum, it must be marked "confidential," and reasonable steps must be taken to ensure its security. Storage in locked cabinets, to which access is limited to those with a need to know, is generally considered a requirement, as are written confidentiality and nondisclosure agreements, executed by all those having access to the information, expressly barring any unauthorized disclosure. At the other extreme, the courts have held that observation of the arrangement of a partially completed chemical processing plant, from an airplane circling overhead, was improper and that reasonable steps to maintain the secret did not necessitate erecting a roof over the whole facility.

Trade secrets are potentially immortal. Their life extends as long as the secret can be maintained. Of course, this also means that they may be extinguished at any moment if the information is disclosed or otherwise becomes available. Disclosure may result from inadvertence ("loose lips sink ships") or improper conduct (ranging from breaches of confidentiality obligations through industrial espionage). Moreover, the information may be discovered or created independently—actually rediscovered or re-created—by another, either by pure happenstance or through analysis or reverse engineering of the products of the trade secret owner or licensees. Herein lies an important difference between patents and trade secrets: An infringer who has independently rediscovered and practiced a patented invention is an infringer nonetheless, but not so with trade secrets. So long as the secret was rediscovered lawfully, through independent research or reverse engineering, once the secret is known, it is no longer a secret, and, therefore, the trade secret protection is lost. For this reason, trade secrets are particularly ill-suited to certain applications. Any information that can be ascertained through product examination will remain a trade secret only for as long as it takes a competitor (or potential licensee) to purchase a sample and inspect it or carry it to an analytical laboratory. As a practical matter, trade secrets are best employed as protection for manufacturing or other processing techniques that are performed in the privacy of one's own (or one's licensee's) facility and that cannot be readily—if at all—discerned from an examination of the product produced thereby.

Trademarks and Service Marks

A *trademark* is a word, symbol, or combination thereof that is used to identify the source, albeit a possibly anonymous source, of goods. Examples of trademarks include Nike, Rolls-Royce, and Kleenex. A *service mark* performs the same function as a trademark with respect to the provision of services. Examples of service marks include FedEx and Roto-Rooter. A trademark or service mark has a potentially perpetual life. Although registration confers several advantages on the owner of a mark, it is not legally required. Registration may be at either the federal or state level. Marks that are unregistered are known as common law marks.

Trademark rights arise out of use. The extent of the use determines the extent of the rights thereby created. Although frequently overlooked, ownership of a mark does not confer rights "in gross." Thus, for example, one owner (General Motors) enjoys the exclusive right to use

CADILLAC as a trademark for automobiles, while another unrelated firm has the same right with respect to dog food.

Proper Trademark Usage— Use it Right or Lose It

If a trademark ceases to serve primarily as an identification of the source of goods and instead comes to identify the goods themselves (i.e., if it becomes the generic term for such goods), the rights to exclusive use of the mark are lost. Notable examples of such lost marks are escalator, thermos, and aspirin. Proper trademark usage is directed to the prevention of such loss. Prior to release, all publications should be reviewed for proper trademark use. (Although the rules of proper trademark usage are beyond the scope of this book, remember: A trademark is an adjective, and should be followed by the appropriate generic term.)

Once a mark is federally registered, it is identified by the symbol ®. The letters TM, or occasionally SM (for service mark), are used to identify unregistered, or common law, marks. Thus, the presence of the designation TM or SM after a mark merely means that someone is claiming proprietary rights thereto, not that the claimant actually *has* such rights. This is not meant, however, to suggest that rights claimed under common law may be safely ignored. Many unregistered marks are extremely strong.

Copyrights

A *copyright* is an exclusionary right. It conveys to its owner the right to prevent others from copying, selling, performing, displaying, or making derivative versions of a work of authorship. The duration of a copyright depends on several factors, but in no event is less than 70 years. (If your planning horizon exceeds 70 years, consult a copyright specialist.) Although registration confers several advantages on the owner of the copyright and is a prerequisite to a suit for copyright infringement, it is not legally required. Prompt registration provides remedies that make a lawsuit affordable. Statutory damages of $150,000 (or more, and attorney fees) for willful infringement can be obtained if published works are registered within three months of publication or if unpublished works are registered before they are infringed.

Copyrights differ from patents in that they only protect against actual copying. A work created by another, without copying, is not an infringement, no matter how similar it may be to a copyrighted work. Moreover, copyright protects only the expression of an idea, not the idea being expressed. Thus, information or data included in a copyrighted work is not protected against appropriation and use by others, although copying of the presentation and arrangement is barred.

Because of their limited scope of protection, copyrights often are overlooked or ignored by businesspeople. Copyrights do, however, have application in the protection of product manuals and instruction booklets, training materials, and marketing and sales publications. More important, copyright has been utilized to protect computer software, although in recent years computer software often has become the subject of patent protection.

Copyright Notice

A copyright notice consists of the symbol ©, or the word "copyright," followed by the year of first publication and the name of the copyright owner. Formerly, publication of a work without a copyright notice caused loss of copyright. For this reason, some people believe that they are free to copy any work that does not bear a copyright notice. *Do not listen to such people.* This aspect of the copyright law was changed more than a decade ago. While a copyright notice remains a requirement if damages are to be recovered from an infringer, the owner of a work published without a notice may obtain an injunction barring further infringement. Thus, the mere absence of a copyright notice does not indicate that a work may be copied freely. Similarly, a copyright notice should be placed on all of one's own works before they are published.

Work for Hire—Sounds Simple, But It Isn't

A *work for hire* is, generally speaking, a work created by an employee within the scope of his or her employment, or, if the parties expressly agree in writing, a work specially commissioned for use as a contribution to a collective work.

The copyright in a work initially vests in the author or authors who created the work. However, in the case of a work for hire, the *employer* is legally considered to be the author. Thus, the copyright of such a work vests in the employer. But what about a work created by a consultant? A consultant is not an employee (If you don't believe this, just ask the Internal Revenue Service.); as a result, the copyright in a work (other than a contribution to a collective work) created by a consultant will vest in the consultant, not in the client. Thus, for example, in the absence of a written copyright assignment, a computer program written by a consultant may be used by the client, but not duplicated or upgraded by the client. (The upgraded program would be a *derivative work.*)

Mask Works

Semiconductor chips, the heart and soul of the electronics age, are produced by a chemical etching process that utilizes a stencil known as a mask work. These chips, which may be very costly to develop, are surprisingly inexpensive to fabricate. The situation positively cries out for copying (known as "piracy" to chip developers and "free enterprise" to chip copiers).

Being useful products, rather than works of authorship, semiconductor chips are not protectable by copyright (although the design drawings of the chips could be so protected). Being functional, mask works cannot be protected by design patents either. Although often complex, the chips frequently lack the nonobviousness required of a utility patent. Moreover, the current pace of technological advancement is such that chips are often obsolete within two years—less than the average period of time to process a patent application in the Patent Office.

To provide intellectual property protection under these trying conditions, Congress passed, in 1984, the Semiconductor Chip Protection Act, creating "a new form of intellectual property" (actually, one closely related to a copyright, with a few patentlike aspects). The act prohibits copying of original mask works that have some degree of originality—they cannot be mere commonplace variations of previous designs. (This is one of the aspects borrowed from patent law.)

Protection is effective upon registration or commercial exploitation (first sale, offer for sale, or other distribution to the public), whichever occurs first. However, such protection terminates two years after exploitation has begun, unless an application for registration has been filed. If registered, protection runs for 10 years from the time it began.

Registered Designs

Many industrial designs pose the same problems with regard to legal protection that are presented by mask works. While novel, they are not nonobvious (and, hence, not protectable by a design patent), and the designs have a commercial or market life that is short relative to the average period of time it takes to process a design patent application in the Patent Office. Not surprisingly, the solution to this problem—design registration—is quite similar to the solution to the comparable problem posed by mask works.

Original designs for useful articles may be registered through a process akin to the registration of a copyright or mask work. The registration must be filed within one year of the first public disclosure of the design, or protection is barred. Protection of the design commences on the earlier of the date of registration or the date the design was first made public and extends for a term of 10 years.

Registration is barred, however, for designs that are dictated solely by utilitarian function, that are commonplace, or that are insignificant variations of commonplace designs.

Noncompetition Agreements and Confidential Disclosure Agreements

Employees (broadly defined) comprise a firm's human capital, a constituent ingredient of intellectual capital. Departing employees deplete a firm's stock of intellectual capital. Worse, they may convey a firm's intellectual capital to a competitor. Indeed, who would value a firm's intellectual capital more highly than its competitors? How, then, is a firm to prevent its intellectual capital from falling into the hands of its competitors? The obvious solution to this problem was barred by the ratification of the Thirteenth Amendment to the Constitution, prohibiting involuntary servitude. The next best solution is the noncompetition agreement.

A noncompetition agreement is a contractual undertaking (lawyer-speak for *agreement*) between an employee and his or her employer. The agreement limits the rights of the employee, upon departure, to accept employment with a competitor of his or her former employer. Noncompetition agreements create a conflict between two public policy considerations; the need of an employer to protect its intellectual capital and the need of a departing employee to secure suitable new employment. Resolution of this conflict is achieved by requiring that the scope of the agreement be limited to that which is clearly necessary to protect the employer, and no more. The limitations are of three kinds: temporal, geographic, and scope.

Temporal limitations refer to the duration of the agreement, that is, the time that must elapse before a departing employee may accept employment with a competitor. The employer's goal is to allow sufficient time for the knowledge held by the departing employee to become obsolete or stale. Obviously, from the employer's perspective, the longer this time period, the better. However, it is wise to remember that the reasonableness of any temporal limitation is a question of fact, to be decided by a jury, and that employees are likely to outnumber employers on any jury. As a practical matter, any period beyond three years is likely to be considered highly suspect.

Geographic limitations refer to the geographic area in which the departing employee may not accept employment with a competitor during the agreed-on time period. Such limitations are based on the premise that the employer's business is limited to a specific geographic market and that the departing employee's activities outside this market area cannot harm the former employer. Geographical limitations work well for purely local businesses, such as beauticians and barbers, dry cleaners, carpenters, and the like; however, given the national, if not global, nature of most business today, there is a serious question as to the continued validity or relevance of this premise. If, however, the employer's business is truly regional, such a limitation may provide a workable means of resolving the conflict.

Finally, *breadth* (also known as scope) limitations refer to the definition of *competitor*. For example, if one is in the plumbing supply business, is "the competition" limited to other plumbing supply companies, or does it include all hardware firms? Today, many firms comprise more than one business. This is especially true in the case of vertically integrated businesses and conglomerates. The competitors of such firms are legion. (Consider, for example, how many firms compete—in one way or another—with some component of General Electric Corporation.) It is necessary, therefore, to define the scope of the prohibition as narrowly as possible. Remember, the goal is merely to prevent the departing employee from utilizing confidential knowledge to the former employer's detriment.

Confidential disclosure agreements, also known as nondisclosure agreements (NDAs), are conceptually related to noncompetition agreements. Each is, in essence, an agreement that the recipient of specified information will use that information only for a specified purpose and will maintain it in confidence. Although public policy issues applicable to noncompetition agreements do not influence nondisclosure agreements, they are subject to certain practical considerations. Because they are so widely used, it is worthwhile to carefully explore and understand these limitations.

Before accepting information in confidence, prospective recipients should assure themselves that the obligations of confidentiality and limited use, at a minimum, will not restrict them from using information already in their possession or information that may subsequently come into their possession from another source, free of any burdens. Obviously, such assurance is difficult, if not impossible, to obtain, in part because recipients often cannot ascertain in advance exactly (1) what information will be disclosed, and (2) what information their firm already possesses. Moreover, lacking prescience, intended recipients have no ability to foresee what information may come into their possession in the future or may be independently developed by their staff.

Excepting certain information from the obligations imposed by the confidential disclosure agreement most commonly solves this problem. Although the precise language utilized may vary somewhat, these exceptions apply to information that:

- Is in the public domain
- Already is in the possession of the recipient
- Subsequently comes into the possession of the recipient, from a source not known by the recipient to be under any obligation of confidentiality
- Is disclosed by the owner of the information to a third party without any obligation of confidentiality
- Subsequently is independently created by the recipient without recourse to the disclosed materials (This last exception is often the subject of some disagreement, as it requires a high degree of trust.)

Notwithstanding the presence of these standard exceptions, the intended recipient should seek as clear—and narrow—as possible a description of the information to be disclosed. Finally, there should be a time limit on the obligation. Ideally, it should expire when the information to be conveyed has become stale. Commonly, confidential disclosure agreements have terms not exceeding three years. See Appendix C for a sample nondisclosure agreement.

Summary

Besides the well-known Big Three of intellectual property—patents, trademarks, and copyrights—the world of IP also consists of trade secrets and know-how; mask works for semiconductor chips; registered designs; noncompetition agreements; and confidential disclosure agreements. Although these forms of IP may seem to differ widely, they all serve a common purpose, which is to protect the advantage that their owner has over the competition by virtue of the IP the company owns.

A patent gives its owner the right to prevent others from making, using, selling, offering for sale, or importing the patented invention.

Patents have effect only within the territory of the country in which they are issued. The three types of patents are plant patents, design patents, and utility patents. The majority of patents are utility patents.

The claims of a patent determine its scope, and these claims are composed of limitations in which the components or steps of the claimed invention are detailed. Every word in a patent claim has meaning and significance, and no two claims can be identical. Patent claims may be either *independent*, meaning that they do not refer to a preceding claim, or *dependent*, meaning that they incorporate by reference the limitations of the claims from which they depend.

Except in certain limited circumstances, a patent application will be published 18 months after its filing date. Once the patent issues, having claims "substantially similar" to those previously published in the patent application, the patentee may recover some damages with respect to infringement that occurred during the period between the publication of the application and the issue of the patent.

A trade secret is information, not generally available, that confers a competitive advantage on its owner. A trade secret's life extends only as long as the secret is maintained and ends as soon as the trade secret is disclosed and the information becomes common knowledge. Hence, care must be taken to maintain their secrecy.

A trademark is a word, symbol, or combination thereof that is used to identify the source of goods. A service mark performs the same role as a trademark with respect to services instead of goods. Both types of marks have a potentially perpetual life, and registration—which may occur on either the state or federal level—is not legally required. Proper trademark usage is important for ensuring that the mark does not become a generic term, such as "aspirin" or "thermos."

A copyright is an exclusionary right that gives its owner the right to prevent others from copying, selling, displaying, performing, or making derivative versions of a work of authorship. The duration of a copyright depends on numerous factors but is no less than 70 years. As with trademarks and service marks, registration is not required, but is a prerequisite to a suit for copyright infringement.

Mask works are stencils used in the production of semiconductor chips. They often are not patented both because they often lack nonobviousness and because the length of time required for the issuance of a patent is often longer than the life span of the chip's technology. Mask works, therefore, are protected by the Semiconductor Chip Protection Act, which prohibits copying of mask works that have some degree of originality.

Registered designs, like mask works, may lack the nonobviousness required for a design patent and may be registered in a process similar to the registration of a mask work or copyright.

Noncompetition agreements and confidential disclosure agreements prevent a firm's departing employees or other recipients of confidential information from using the firm's intellectual capital themselves or selling it to a competitor.

CHAPTER 4

Licensing Strategies: The Carrot and the Stick

After reading this chapter you will be able to

- Understand the difference between "carrot licensing" and "stick licensing"
- Recognize the advantages and disadvantages of both exclusive and nonexclusive licenses
- Understand what a joint venture is, and how it can help an IP owner capitalize on its IP
- Recognize how a strategic alliance works

Carrot Licensing

A license taken by a party under no compulsion to do so is a "voluntary" (this is a euphemism, not a quote) license, also known as a carrot license. The owner of intellectual property (IP) has held out a carrot, in the form of benefits to be realized from the use of the property, and a prospective user has decided to take the carrot by adapting and utilizing the property and, more important from the viewpoint of the owner, paying for such use.

Picture a mule harnessed to a cart. The mule is lethargic and stubborn and has no interest in pulling the cart. The cart's driver has attached a carrot to a pole and seeks to induce the mule to pull the cart by dangling the carrot just beyond the mule's reach. In order for the inducement to succeed, the carrot must be attractive to the mule. Unless and until the mule desires the carrot, the cart goes nowhere. So it is with "voluntary" licensing. No progress is made until the offeree perceives the desirability of the property being offered.

Many inventors are so taken by their creations that they assume that the merits thereof are readily apparent to all. Such inventors are wrong. Most large corporations react according to the laws of physics—the greater the mass, the greater the inertia. Many are indeed akin to the mule—lethargic and stubborn—while some are simply jackasses. They (both the mules and the jackasses) will present a myriad of reasons why the proffered property is of no value to them.

IN THE REAL WORLD

NIHS

Most of the corporate world is afflicted by NIHS—the not invented here syndrome. This makes carrot licensing a tough business.

The Iron Fist Within the Velvet Glove

A mule may desire the carrot but nevertheless will not pull the cart if it perceives that the carrot is within its reach. It must be convinced that only by pulling the cart will it be able to reach the carrot. So it is with prospective licensees. After they have been sold on the desirability of the proffered property, they must be convinced that their use of the property is contingent on their payment for such use. A potential licensee that believes that the owner of the property is unwilling or unable to enforce its rights therein will use the property without taking a license (miserable, lowlife infringers) or will pay only a token amount (scum-sucking chiselers). Thus, no license is truly "voluntary." It is the implicit threat of legal action that induces offerees to take licenses and pay realistic royalties (more on this fascinating topic in Chapter 9). To quote Al Capone, "You can go a long way with a smile. You can go a lot further with a smile and a gun."

Stick Licensing

Occasionally (actually, all too often), some lousy, misbegotten bottom feeder is found infringing the IP of another. If the wretched slug is taken to task (sued or threatened with suit) by the property owner, and thereupon indicates a desire to continue his heretofore nefarious activities under honorable terms, a license may be granted by the offended owner. Such a license, taken involuntarily, under explicit threat of legal action, is known as a stick license. If the proffered license is not taken, the property owner may utilize the courts to righteously beat the infringer with the noble stick of his or her IP rights.

Ironically, stick licensing is generally more profitable and less difficult than carrot licensing. Carrot licensing consists of two steps, the first of which is to educate the prospective licensee as to the desirability of the proffered IP—that is, to teach the mule to like carrots. In stick licensing, this step has been completed before the parties make contact. No sales or educational effort is required of the property owner—the mule has, in effect, taught itself. Moreover, the low-down, slimy toad of an infringer has already committed itself to use of the subject property. Specialized plant and equipment may have been purchased, advertising and promotional materials may have been prepared, orders may have been taken. None of the risks and uncertainties inherent in a carrot license (how much investment is required, will it work, will it sell) remains. To the contrary, the investment already has been made and the results have proven successful. The infringer is thus in a poor negotiating position. All of its investment may be lost if a license is not secured.

Exclusive versus Nonexclusive Licenses

An *exclusive license* is one that grants rights to the licensee to the exclusion of all others. This is to be distinguished from a *sole license*, which grants rights to the licensee to the exclusion of all save the licensor. The distinction is one of great importance—the grant of an exclusive license puts the licensor out of business, to the extent of the license. Note the last phase of the preceding sentence, "to the extent of the license." Exclusive licenses are commonly thought to convey all of the licensor's rights, leaving the licensor with only a bare ownership interest in this licensed property. (See Chapter 5 for an important feature of such a license.) Frequently this is so, but not necessarily. Some licenses, known as limited exclusive licenses, are exclusive only in limited respects. Such a license may be exclusive with respect to a defined geographic area (e.g., a trademark licensed for use only in the state of Texas), or with respect to less than all of the property owned by the licensor (e.g., a U.S. patent on an improved automobile transmission licensed for use only on vehicles with engines of less than 200 horsepower). Some licensees are exclusive for an initial period and then become nonexclusive.

As would be expected, most licensees would prefer to have a monopoly in the licensed property and will pay a premium to secure it. As a result, an exclusive license generally commands a higher price than a nonexclusive license of the same property. This is not to say, however, that a licensor always should seek to grant an exclusive license in preference to a nonexclusive one. An exclusive license yields only a single royalty (albeit one that may include periodic "running royalty" payments), while a property licensed on a nonexclusive basis may garner royalties from a number of licensees. When choosing a licensing approach, many licensors consider only one question: Will the sum of the royalties from a number of nonexclusive licensees exceed the royalty from a single exclusive licensee? This is overly simplistic. It ignores issues of risk and control.

With an exclusive license, the licensor has put all of its eggs in one basket. A breach of the license contract, a bankruptcy or other financial problems, mismanagement or interruption of the licensee's business, or any of a host of other problems may cause a reduction, or total loss, of revenues from a license. With a program of nonexclusive licensing, there will be a number of licensees. Hence, the probability that at least one of them will encounter difficulties is many times greater than the corresponding probability of a problem with a single exclusive licensee. However, while a problem with one of the nonexclusive licenses may result in a diminution in the revenue stream, a similar problem with an exclusive license may result in a total loss of revenue. (We are assuming that all licenses, both exclusive and nonexclusive, include a running royalty.)

IN THE REAL WORLD

Exceptions to the "Exclusive" Rule

Most carrot licenses tend to be exclusive, because they require a substantial investment and risk taking on the part of the licensee. A notable example occurs in the pharmaceutical industry, where most new drugs are licensed on an exclusive basis.

It has been said that when you borrow $500 from a bank, you become a debtor, but when you borrow $5,000,000, you become a partner in the bank. A similar result obtains in licensing. With several nonexclusive licensees, none has much influence, and the power of control rests in the hands of the licensor. An exclusive licensee, however, wields substantial power, both financial and legal (see Chapter 5).

Thus, a licensor wishing to retain control and wishing to limit exposure to loss (as opposed to risk or probability of loss) may well prefer a program of nonexclusive licensing. This is not to suggest that exclusive licensing is without advantages. Clearly, license administration is facilitated when there is only one licensee to monitor.

Joint Ventures and Research and Development Collaboration Agreements

Nothing Ventured, Nothing Gained

The situation may arise that the IP owner wishes to capitalize on this property yet lacks an essential element to do so. For example, the property owner may have insufficient manufacturing capacity or may lack an effective channel of distribution. The property owner may believe that marketing muscle, in the form of a well-recognized trademark or service mark, would be necessary to get the new product (or service) off the ground. If another firm can supply the missing element, a *joint venture* may be an effective vehicle for commercializing the property.

Basically, a joint venture is an entity, such as a partnership or corporation, created for a specific limited purpose and owned by two or more parties. The contributions or investments of each of the joint venturers (owners) are usually in kind, not in cash. In this instance, the IP owner would contribute the intellectual property, either by assignment or license, while the other venturers would contribute, perhaps, appropriate manufacturing or distribution services and a trademark or service mark (again, either by assignment or license). It is hoped that the whole is greater than the sum of its parts. (If it is not, then a joint venture is not the way to go.)

Because a joint venture is a separate entity, it allows its owners to continue their own existence with minimal interference. Most often the joint venture is dissolved when its purpose is accomplished. For this reason, it is especially important that the parties agree, during its formation, on a plan of termination, including a decision as to the future ownership of any IP created by the joint venture itself.

A strategic alliance differs from a joint venture primarily in that it is not a separate entity. Rather, it is simply an agreement between its various members (the allies) to cooperate in some specified manner. Generally, the allies offer each other preferential, or exclusive, terms with respect to the sale of goods or the provision of services. Most commonly the goods or services subject to the agreement are those in which the supplier enjoys some competitive advantage. The alliances are constituted so that each member receives, under most favorable terms, those goods or services it needs to enable it to most effectively capitalize on its own area of strength or comparative advantage. Because it is not an entity, a strategic alliance cannot develop or hold IP. For this reason, dissolution or expiration of a strategic alliance presents few of the problems inherent in the termination of a joint venture.

Summary

A license may either be voluntary (a "carrot" license) or involuntary (a "stick" license). Carrot licenses, where the patent owner must convince the prospective licensee that the proffered IP is both valuable and viable, are much more difficult to sell to prospective licensees than are stick licenses, where the prospective licensee is an infringer already using the intellectual property and thus already aware of the value of the property.

An exclusive license grants the use of the IP to one licensee to the exclusion of all others, even the licensor. A sole license allows only the licensee and the licensor the rights to use of the IP. A licensor may grant any number of nonexclusive licenses, but, since such a license does not secure a monopoly for the licensee, it generally commands a lower price than does an exclusive license. However, nonexclusive licenses have two advantages over exclusive licenses: (1) multiple nonexclusive licenses provide multiple sources of revenue as opposed to the single source of revenue provided by an exclusive license; and (2) multiple nonexclusive licenses dilute the influence each licensee may exert over the licensor.

A joint venture is created for a specific limited purpose and owned by two or more parties. The contribution of each of the joint venturers consists of IP or services such as manufacturing or distribution. A joint venture forms a separate entity, which may own intellectual property.

A strategic alliance is an agreement between its various members to cooperate in some specified manner, and is not a separate entity. Allies agree to offer each other goods or services on preferential or exclusive terms.

CHAPTER 5

Patent Licenses

After reading this chapter you will be able to

- Understand the key issues peculiar to a patent license

- Verify that the license gives you the rights that you *think* it does

- Understand how the doctrine of "implied license" ensures that the licensee receives something of value in return for payment of royalties

- Recognize why "patent marking" is important

- Discern when patent enforcement is a good idea and when it may not be worth the time and expense—and how to decide who pays for it (the licensor or the licensee)

- Understand what happens at the termination of a license

- Determine what happens if a licensed patent is found invalid or unenforceable

- Appreciate why allowing a licensee to make improvements on the licensed patent(s) can be a *good* thing

C ongratulations! You have just received a patent on an Improved Mousetrap (this is a typical patent title as authored by creative patent draftspeople). Prospective licensees are beating the proverbial path to your door. You are about to embark on a licensing campaign to "monetize" (the current buzzword meaning "to make money from") the patent.

It is thus time to focus on the specific issues presented by a patent license.

Definitions

A Rose by Any Other Name

The words and phrases requiring definition in a patent license will, of course, depend on the circumstances and the draftsperson. At a minimum, however, the following must be defined: Licensed Patents, Licensed Products, and Territory. These definitions do not merely define words or phrases; they, in fact, define the scope of the license.

 TIPS & TECHNIQUES

Hint: Defined terms are identified by capital letters. If a word or phrase is capitalized, it may not mean what you think it does. Check the Definitions section of the agreement to be sure of the term's meaning.

"Licensed Patents" are those that are the subject of a license. The license may comprise several patents or only a single one. In addition to the patents enumerated in the definition, it is quite common to include the phrase "and any continuations, continuations-in-part, divisions and reissues thereof." This inclusion is intended to ensure that any future patent(s) arising out of the patent application(s) that mature into the enumerated patent(s) are included in the license, along with any patents resulting from the correction of any enumerated patent (the reissues). Such a provision is merely a matter of prudence and, except in unusual circumstances, entirely appropriate. Sometimes, however, the provision is expanded to include "and any foreign equivalents or any foreign patents claiming the benefit thereof." This latter is no longer a mere prudence; it is a significant broadening of the definition. The intentional inclusion of foreign patent rights in a license is fine; the inadvertent inclusion, resulting from the addition of "standard language" to a draft license by a helpful (euphemism for "shady") prospective licensee, is not. Be careful with the definition of Licensed Patents.

"Licensed Products" are those that may be produced, used, offered for sale, sold, or imported by the licensee under the terms of the license. Licensed Products may, at one extreme, include "any product covered by one or more claims of any of the Licensed Patents." In order to prevent a licensee from later denying that its products are covered by licensed patent claims (and thus avoiding the payment of running royalties with respect thereto), it is prudent to add (when known) "including, but not limited to, the following products: (list product or model numbers)." (It also may be advantageous to include a provision for the arbitration—rather than litigation—of any dispute that may arise as to whether any new product subsequently introduced by the licensee is subject to a royalty obligation.)

At the other end of the spectrum, Licensed Products may comprise only a single, specified product or model. Between these two (2) (note legal writing style) extremes lies the opportunity for creative licensing. The monopoly rights secured by the patent can be apportioned out in ways limited only by the imagination of the parties. Virtually any product parameter may be used as a basis for apportionment. By clever division of the potential uses of the Licensed Patents, it is possible to simultaneously grant exclusive licenses—albeit for limited fields of use—to several licensees. Given that exclusive licenses generally bear higher royalty rates than nonexclusive licenses, the advantages of such an approach should be obvious to the prospective licensor.

Having defined *what* is being licensed (the Licensed Patents) and *how* it may be used (in Licensed Products), there remains the question of *where* it may be used. This question is answered by the definition of the "Territory." Like Licensed Products, Territory may be defined broadly or narrowly. At the broad extreme, the Territory may encompass the entire country (or countries) where Licensed Patents are in effect. Thus, for example, Territory may be defined as simply "the United States, its territories and possessions." At the narrow extreme, Territory may be limited to a single location, such as "Licensee's business establishment located at [*street address*]."

Occasionally a prospective corporate licensee will seek to have a license that extends to its "affiliates." Sometimes the request is made quite explicitly. Sometimes the phrase "and its affiliates" is merely slipped into a draft of the license. The impact of such an inclusion depends on the circumstances. (The moral impact of any attempted sleight of hand is another matter.) If the license bears a running royalty, the sudden appearance of additional licensed parties may be of little moment. If, however, a fixed fee license is contemplated, such an appearance would be most unwelcome, as the newcomer would, in effect, be receiving a free license. When contemplating a fixed fee license, the prudent (euphemism for "not gullible") licensor will limit the license grant to current affiliates of the prospective licensee or to those identified by the licensee and listed in the license agreement.

TIPS & TECHNIQUES

It is a misuse of a patent—a misuse that will render it unenforceable—to seek to enforce it beyond its terms. Thus, a license should not require the payment of royalties in respect of sales occurring after the expiration of the licensed patent (or the last to expire of multiple licensed patents), or in respect of activities that occur outside of the territory of the nation that issued the patent(s).

Grant

Reading Your Rights

The various rights secured by a patent need not be licensed together. They may be licensed separately. A patentee may, for example, license another to make and use a patented device, but not to sell it. The ability to license the various rights separately is, however, limited by the doctrine of "implied license," which is founded on the legal principle that contracts are to be construed so as to give effect to the intent of the parties, coupled with the logical corollary that the parties must have intended that the licensee receive something of value in exchange for the payment of a royalty (see "failure of consideration" in Chapter 2). Consider a license that limited the licensee to only making a patented article—allowing neither use nor sale. Under the express terms of such a license, the licensee could not possibly profit from the authorized production of the articles, as they were both useless and unsalable. If this license were litigated (as it surely would be, when the licensee woke up to its predicament), the court certainly would decide that the license included (at a minimum) the "implied" right to sell the articles if the licensee was, for example, in the business of manufacturing and selling such articles, or to use them, if the licensee typically used such articles in the course of its business.

A related issue arises where the licensee lacks the ability to, itself, manufacture the patented article. In such a case, the licensee normally (if it had the foresight) would request authorization to have the patented articles made for it by another party. This authorization generally is effectuated by the inclusion of the phrase "have made" in the enumeration of rights in the Grant, although, strictly speaking, it conceptually comprises a limited sublicense to the actual manufacturer. A licensee should not rely on implication with respect to the right to have the patented article made by an unlicensed third party. If this right is desired, it should be expressly included in the Grant.

A licensor, however, should consider carefully the possible implications of a right to "have made" before including it in a license. Consider a potential licensee that will be selling a patented article. The potential licensee, a small firm, seeks a paid-up license and, based on its size, suggests a commensurately small royalty. If the license limits the licensee to those articles it actually makes "in-house," the proposed paid-up license may be acceptable. If, however, the license allows the licensee to have patented articles made for it by others, it is, in effect, no longer a small firm. If it can have articles produced by third parties, the licensee is, effectively, of unlimited capacity. Such licensees may function as middlemen between manufacturers that wish to produce the patented articles (without paying a royalty) and their customers. Such a situation is acceptable—but only if the license has a running royalty. Licensors should consider carefully before including the right to "have made" in a paid-up license.

An exclusive license, like membership in an exclusive club, offers certain special privileges. The notable privilege associated with an exclusive patent license is standing to bring suit for infringement of the licensed patent(s). Upon the grant of a truly exclusive license—one that effectively transfers all of the patentee's rights to the licensee—standing to sue passes from the patentee to the licensee. This aspect of an exclusive license, the loss of control of the licensed patent(s), should be borne in mind when weighing the choice between exclusive and nonexclusive licensing.

Another privilege that may be accorded a licensee is the right to grant sublicenses. The grant of such a privilege should be tightly controlled (i.e., all sublicenses should be subject to the approval of the licensor). The licensee/sublicensor should, however, remain responsible for the sublicensee's proper and full compliance with all of the terms and conditions of the license. Most significantly, if the sublicensee defaults in the payment of royalties—tough! Payment is due from the licensee/sublicensor.

Patent Marking Provisions

Making Your Mark

Before damages can be collected from a patent infringer, the patentee must establish that the infringer was warned or notified of the infringement. Once notified, damages accrue from the date of the notice. Notice may be either "actual" or "constructive." Actual notice is about what it would seem—a letter from the patentee, identifying both the patent and the infringing products and including a clear statement that the patent covered the products, or, equivalently, that the products infringed the patent. Constructive notice, with respect to a commercialized patent, comprises marking the patented product (or, if impractical, its packaging) with the patent number(s). For patents that are not commercialized, or where the commercialization does not yield a markable product, the marking requirement is excused. If, however, a product that could be marked is commercialized without the appropriate patent marking, damages in respect of infringement begin to accrue only when the infringer is placed on actual notice.

The marking requirement applies not only to the patentee, but to licensees as well. A licensee's failure to mark carries the same penalty as a failure by the patentee. It is, therefore, extremely important to a patentee that all licenses include provisions requiring the licensees to mark licensed products with the relevant patent numbers and that the licensees comply with these requirements. Some prospective licensees may object to inclusion of a marking provision in their license. Before acceding to demands that such provision be omitted or deleted, the prospective licensor should consider carefully the implications of such acquiescence, namely, the need to give actual notice to infringers before damages begin to accrue. Occasionally someone will suggest circumventing this problem through the use of a "covenant not to sue" rather than a license. *Do not do this.* A covenant not to sue is the legal equivalent of a license, as is any other form of agreement under which a party is able to utilize a patented invention free of legal action for infringement.

TIPS & TECHNIQUES

Non-exclusive license = Covenant not to sue

Patent Enforcement

A patent licensee is paying for the privilege of utilizing the patented invention and is, therefore, likely to become exceedingly irate on discovering that a competitor is utilizing the same invention for free (i.e., infringing the licensed patent). Typically, on making such a discovery, the disgruntled licensee vociferously demands that the licensor take *prompt action* (lawyerspeak for "run out and file a lawsuit") against the unscrupulous, misbegotten son of a diseased camel. Indeed, a prospective licensee may seek to insert, in the license, a requirement that the patentee enforce the licensed patents against any infringer. This requirement is known as abating infringement (also as enriching the attorneys).

Simply put, patent infringement is costly. A patentee should not lightly assume a potentially unlimited enforcement obligation. An infringer's activities may be *de minimus* (Latin term meaning "not worth bothering about") such that enforcement efforts are not economically justified. Also, there may be a difference of opinion between a licensee—which maintains that a competitor is infringing—and the patentee—which believes that the accused activities do not constitute infringement. The patentee should avoid granting the licensee the right to decide when an infringement action will be brought.

From the perspective of the patentee, enforcement of the licensed patent should be optional, not obligatory. Obviously, a patentee that does undertake enforcement should retain whatever recovery is had from the infringer. Where a patentee is compelled to accept an enforcement obligation, it may seek to have the licensee pay all, or at least a portion, of the costs incurred. (Licensees are notably less enthusiastic about suing alleged infringers when they themselves must bear the expense.) A licensee that shares in paying enforcement costs should, logically and equitably, be entitled to a corresponding share of any recovery.

IN THE REAL WORLD

The Cost of Litigation

Presently, the median cost of patent litigation in the United States is around $2 million.

From the perspective of the licensee, payment of a royalty creates an entitlement to freedom from unlicensed competition. It is, therefore, the obligation of the patentee to sue promptly all known infringers. As a means of motivating the patentee to prosecute vigorously such lawsuits, the licensee may seek a provision that no royalties will accrue while the infringement continues. Under some licenses, the patentee has the option—not the obligation—to enforce the licensed patent against infringers. In such cases, the licensee should seek the right to itself enforce the patent should the patentee decline to do so and to retain any recovery resulting from its efforts.

It is important to note that enforcement of a patent is limited to those with "standing" (lawyerspeak for "the legal right to sue"). Only the patentee(s) or, if an exclusive license has been granted, the exclusive licensee has standing to sue for patent infringement. Nonexclusive licensees do not have standing; they can sue only by joining the patentee as a plaintiff.

Term and Termination

It is a misuse of a patent to attempt to license it beyond its term. Such an attempt may render the patents unenforceable. While any shorter period is allowable, the term of most patent licenses extends to the expiration of the licensed patent or, where multiple patents are included in a single license, to the expiration of the last patent to expire.

In the special case of an exclusive license, however, the license term (but not the accrual of a running royalty) may extend beyond the patent expiration date, so as to allow the exclusive licensee to conclude any litigation against infringers. While the term of the license is, in such cases, extended, royalties cease to accrue upon expiration of the licensed patents.

The definition of "Term" is generally included in the Definitions section of the license. The license may, however, terminate before the end of its term. Termination may occur, for example, if one of the parties (most likely the licensee) has materially breached the license agreement and has failed to timely cure the breach after notice by the nonbreaching party. Circumstances that will or may result in termination of the license are set forth in a clause or section that is typically identified as "Termination." Among the provisions typically found in the Termination clause are those pertaining to the disposal of any inventory of Licensed Product on hand when the license is terminated. Most commonly, the licensee is allowed to sell any such inventory, complete any work in process, and fill any existing contracts, subject to the obligation to pay the appropriate royalty.

Representations and Warranties

Frequently, a prospective licensee will request that the patentee warrant that the licensed patents are valid and enforceable and that the manufacture, use, sale, offer for sale, or importation of Licensed Products (as that term is defined in the license agreement) will not infringe the rights of any third party. Some prospective licensees go even further, demanding that the patentee warrant that "use of the patented invention" will not infringe any third-party rights. Such demands are unreasonable and, for any sentient patentee, unacceptable. It is virtually impossible to identify all of the relevant prior art, and, hence, it is virtually impossible to be assured of the validity of a patent. Potentially invalidating prior art comprises not only prior patents, both domestic and foreign, but also printed publications from around the world, as well as public activities within the United States. At most, a patentee can represent that it is *presently unaware* of any prior art—or, indeed, any reason that would render the licensed patent invalid. It is, similarly, virtually impossible to be aware of all of the various property rights—utility patents, design patents, registered designs, copyrights, trade secrets, and trade dress—that might be asserted by some third party. Again, at most, the patentee can represent that it is *presently unaware* of any third-party rights that would be infringed.

The patentee, likewise, cannot reasonably make any representation with respect to the licensees' freedom to use the "licensed invention" for the simple reason that the precise manner of such use is not defined. There is undoubtedly any number of possible products on which the claims of the licensed patent might read and that the licensee may, in the future, produce. The patentee is, in effect, being asked to certify that none of these possible licensed products—the specifics of which are unknown to the patentee—infringes any property right of any third party. This is beyond impossible; it is insane.

Lastly, a prospective licensee may request a warranty (colloquially known as an anti-sandbagging provision) that the licensor has no other patent which would be infringed by licensee's actions under the license. A request of this nature is not unreasonable and might well be granted by the licensor. Nevertheless, a licensor that might expect to acquire additional patents in the future may wish to limit itself to a representation that it *presently* has no other such patent. A closely related issue, the right to use any improvements to the licensed invention, is discussed later in this chapter.

Patent Invalidity or Unenforceability

Unlike the Pope, the United States Patent and Trademark Office is not infallible. Some issued patents are subsequently determined to be invalid or unenforceable. What is the effect of such a determination on a license? The answer to this question depends, in part, on the number of patents included in the license. If a license is to a single patent, the invalidity or unenforceability of that patent should result in termination of the license, thereby relieving the licensee of any further royalty obligations (if the royalty was prepaid—a "paid-up license"—oops!). If, however, the license is to more than one patent and the determination of invalidity or unenforceability is to less than all of them, the answer is not so clear or simple. The license continues as to the remaining licensed patent or patents (those not found invalid or unenforceable), but what of the running royalty? Like most questions in the law, that depends. In this case, it may remain the same, or it may be reduced, depending on the provisions of the license. If the parties have made provision for such an eventuality, that provision will control. If there is no such provision, but there is a provision as to the effect of the expiration of one of multiple-licensed patents, such provision probably will be applied to the similar circumstances of the invalidity or unenforceability of one or more of the licensed patents. If there is no provision as to the effects of either expiration or invalidity, for shame! Such is the stuff of which litigation is made.

Improvements

The ocean tides wait for no man. Neither do the tides of technological progress. The newly patented invention of today is the mature product of tomorrow and the obsolete closeout of next week. The antidote to this perpetual aging and decay is constant refinement and improvement.

A licensee may request that rights to any improvements of the Licensed Patents subsequently made by the patentee be included in the license. Typically, such a request does not contemplate any increase in the royalty, and, for this reason, some patentees resist the idea. In the case of a paid-up license, the patentee's reluctance to include further rights in the license is reasonable. Why license additional rights without additional compensation? If, however, the license in question will bear a running royalty, such reluctance may be ill-advised (euphemism for "dumb"). Use of the improvements should enable the licensee to achieve greater sales. The increased sales will result in greater royalty payments to the patentee. Moreover, any patent(s) on the improvements will expire after the expiration of the patent(s) on the original or basic invention(s). Thus, inclusion of rights to the use of future improvements serves to extend the term of the license.

A licensee is, of course, free to use its own improvements (i.e., those that it created or developed). Some licensors have sought to compel licensees to assign all rights to any improvement made by the licensee to the licensor. There is a body of law that suggests this may comprise an antitrust violation. For this reason, it is now more common for licensors merely to request a nonexclusive license of any such improvement, allowing the licensor to retain ownership.

Miscellaneous

Product liability laws are far-reaching, and the creativity of plaintiffs' lawyers knows no bounds. Therefore, although it is unlikely that a patent licensor will be held legally responsible for any injury or damage caused by the products or services of a licensee, it is nevertheless universal practice to demand indemnification for any such claims. For a more complete discussion of indemnification and product liability insurance, see Chapter 7.

Summary

As a form of contract, a patent license has several basic parts that must be structured carefully to ensure that the rights and intent of both the licensee and the licensor will be maintained. Defined terms are usually capitalized and should be scrutinized carefully—make sure they mean what you intend them to mean. Special attention should be paid to the terms "Licensed Patents," "Licensed Products," and "Territory."

The various rights associated with a patent may be licensed separately, but the patentee's ability to do this is limited by the doctrine of implied license, which helps to ensure that the licensee receives adequate rights in exchange for royalties paid.

When a patent is being infringed, the infringer must be put on notice—either actual (the patentee informs the infringer of the infringement via a letter) or constructive (the patentee marks the patented product with the patent number)—before the patentee can collect damages.

Damages accrue from the date of notice. For this reason, it is very important that the patentee and any licensees mark any patented products with the patent number(s); otherwise, damages in respect of infringement begin only when the infringer is placed on actual notice.

A patentee should consider carefully who will have the right to decide when to enforce the licensed patent(s) against infringers—and who should bear the cost of such enforcement. Licensees may be less adamant about suing every infringer if they must share (or bear) the expense.

The term, i.e., duration, of a license is usually found in the Definitions section of the license. However, the license may terminate before the end of its term if one of the parties breaches the license agreement and fails to cure the breach in a timely manner. The Termination clause or section of the agreement sets forth the circumstances that will result in termination as well as what becomes of any inventory of the Licensed Product after the license terminates.

In the Representations and Warranties section, the patentee must carefully avoid warranting that there is no prior art or any other reason that would invalidate the patent(s). It is virtually impossible to know this for certain, or to know if there are any other third-party rights that may be infringed. The patentee should state simply that it is unaware of such infringement or invalidating factors.

The license should make provisions for the possibility that one or more of the licensed patents will be found invalid or unenforceable.

Giving the licensee rights to use any improvements to the licensed patent(s) made by the licensee can prove advantageous to the licensor, sometimes generating greater royalty payments and extending the term of the license.

CHAPTER 6

Know-how and Trade Secret Licenses

After reading this chapter you will be able to

- Define the licensed trade secrets and know-how in a license agreement

- Understand why the licensee of this type of intellectual property needs to be especially sure that the license provides sufficient disclosures to enable it to utilize the licensed property effectively

- Discern what the licensor should be careful to avoid in such a license

- Understand what may happen when the licensed trade secret or know-how ceases to be secret and what constitutes "public knowledge" for purposes of a license agreement

- Maintain the secrecy of the property once it is licensed and after the termination of the license

The complexities of licensing know-how and trade secrets arise, in large part, from the fragility of their existence. It is not the underlying information but the secrecy that creates the value of such properties. If the secrecy is lost, so too is the value. This is not to say that licensees (and others) would not continue to use such information after it became publicly known. They most certainly would; however, they would not continue to pay for that use.

Definitions

In a patent license, the licensed property is fully defined in the patent document itself. The licensee receives rights in respect of the invention disclosed and claimed in the licensed patent. Trade secrets and know-how are often not so readily defined. Rather, they may take the form of a vast collection of related materials, including plans, drawings, specifications, formulas, procedures, process descriptions, lists of materials, and lists of vendors, all of which should enable the licensee to accomplish some desired objective, and all of which are to be delivered to the licensee upon execution of the license. Not infrequently (note the lawyerly use of double negatives), demonstrations, training, or other technical assistance also are provided by the licensor.

It is incumbent on the licensee to assure that it receives sufficient disclosure and assistance to enable it to utilize the licensed property properly and effectively. Indeed, the licensee may wish to define the required disclosure and level of assistance as that which will enable it to effectively utilize the licensed trade secrets and know-how. Such a definition comprises an open-ended commitment on the part of the licensor and, in effect, a warranty that the licensee *will* be able to effectively utilize the licensed property.

A licensor may well prefer to place limits on the amount of assistance, if any, to be provided to the licensee, or to require payment for any assistance beyond a specified level. A licensee may seek to negotiate for the provision of such assistance as may prove necessary and make suitable provision in the license agreement. While the desirability of providing assistance is obvious, the licensor should seek to avoid anything that could be construed as a warranty as to the suitability or effectiveness of the licensed property. One means of avoiding such an implied warranty situation is to have the prospective licensor define the licensed property with reference to a list of the items of information—but not the information itself—to be disclosed to the licensee pursuant to the license.

In those situations where the prospective licensee has had access to the secret information prior to execution of the license—subject, it is hoped, to a suitable confidential disclosure agreement—the license may simply acknowledge receipt of the licensed property.

Unlike a patent, which has effect only in the country of issue, a secret is a secret the world over. Thus, the potential geographic scope of a know-how or trade secret license is worldwide. Also unlike patents, which have a limited term, the life span of trade secrets and know-how is potentially unlimited. A license of trade secrets and know-how may have a term of a fixed period, or it may continue for so long as the licensee continues to utilize the licensed property.

What happens if the secrets become publicly known? The answer to that question depends on the termination provisions in the license agreement. If the license provides for termination by the licensee in the event that the licensed properties become publicly known, the licensee may invoke this provision to terminate the license. Then, utilizing the now publicly known information, the now ex-licensee may continue as before—but without paying any royalties. If, however, the license does not provide for termination upon loss of secrecy, the licensee may be obligated to continue to pay royalties for use of information now widely and freely available. Such a calamity befell Warner-Lambert (W-L), the licensee of the trade secret formula for Listerine antiseptic. When the secret formula ceased to be secret, W-L deemed the license terminated and ceased to pay royalties, but continued to sell product made in accordance with the now publicly known recipe. The licensor's estate sued for breach of contract. The court found that W-L was obliged to honor its covenant to pay royalties for the sale of product made in accord with

TIPS & TECHNIQUES

The licensee of a trade secret should insist on an explicit provision allowing termination of the license in the event the licensed trade secret becomes freely available.

the formula, there being no provision in the license allowing termination by the licensee while the formula—secret or not—was still in use.

A similar problem may arise when an inventor, having filed a patent application in respect of an invention, seeks to license the invention without waiting for the pending patent application to mature into an issued patent. Such was the situation in the famous (or infamous) Quickpoint case (see "In the Real World: *Aronson v. Quick Point Pencil Co.*")

IN THE REAL WORLD

Aronson v. Quick Point Pencil Co.

In the Quick Point case (Aronson v. Quick Point Pencil Co., 440 U.S. 257 [1979]), the inventor of a key chain filed a patent application and licensed her trade secret rights and rights to her future patent to a manufacturer. The license was to terminate upon the expiration of the patent. The invention was, however, found by the Patent Office to be unpatentable and no patent issued. Hence, there was no patent expiration. The nature of the invention was such as to be readily discerned on inspection of the key chain. Thus, no secret survived the introduction of the product into the market. The manufacturer eventually tired of paying royalties—but not of selling the key chains. The licensor sued for breach of contract and won. The court held that the licensee had received the advantage for which it had bargained—the opportunity to be the first to sell the subject key chain—and, therefore, was obligated to pay royalties on all its sales until the occurrence of the agreed, albeit now-nonexistent, expiration date.

TIPS & TECHNIQUES

When entering a license of trade secrets, know-how, or an invention that is the subject of a pending patent application, consider the possibility that the secret will become publicly known or that the subject matter of the patent application will prove to be unpatentable (or that the issued patent claims will not read on, i.e., cover, the structures or processes of interest to the licensee) and make provision accordingly.

Confidentiality

My Lips Are Sealed

Obviously, maintenance of secrecy is critical to the value of trade secrets and know-how. Therefore, any license of such property should include suitable provisions directed toward the preservation of confidentiality. At a minimum, a licensee should accord the licensed property the same degree of care and caution afforded its own confidential or proprietary information. Ideally, access to the licensed property should be limited to those with a "need to know," and all such individuals should execute agreements acknowledging the confidential nature of the information and their duty to maintain it in confidence. More important, the licensee (and, if possible, all individuals with access to the confidential information) should acknowledge that unauthorized or unintended disclosure thereof would cause irreparable harm, that the loss engendered by such disclosure could not be adequately compensable in money, and that the parties therefore stipulate to the prompt entry of preliminary and permanent injunctions barring such disclosure, in addition to such other remedies as may be appropriate.

As a general rule, the obligations of the parties are extinguished by the expiration or termination of a license. The obligation to maintain confidentiality should be a noteworthy exception to this rule. It should be made clear in a license (any license, not only licenses of trade secrets and know-how) that the obligation of confidentiality survives termination of the license for any reason.

Assignability

When all is said and done, a promise is no better than the party that made it. A licensor, having entrusted valued and valuable secrets to a licensee, would not wish to discover suddenly that the license had been assigned to a stranger who now possessed the very secrets the licensor sought so diligently to protect. To avoid such an unpleasant surprise, a trade secret or know-how licensor is well advised to prohibit any assignment of the license. Failing in that, assignment should be conditioned on the written approval of the licensor (which approval, of course, would not be unreasonably withheld).

Termination—With Extreme Prejudice

The prudent (euphemism meaning "not an idiot") licensee will request (actually demand) a provision for termination of the license in the event the licensed property becomes publicly known. The question remains, however, of what is the appropriate measure of such public knowledge. Know-how is most commonly a collection and compilation of information that is already known to the public. The same description often may apply to trade secrets. An unprincipled (euphemism for "despicable cheat") licensee, once conversant with the details of the licensed property, may attempt to reconstruct it from various publicly available sources, so as to establish that it is no longer confidential. This, of course, would present the unscrupulous worm with the opportunity to terminate the license—and the royalty payments—while continuing to utilize the "publicly known" information. In order to prevent such sharp practice (lawyerspeak for "thievery"), the licensor should qualify the term "publicly known" by specifying that it be "from a single source." Unless all of the licensed property is found in a single, publicly available source, it is not "publicly known."

What's Mine Is Mine

Lest the point escape the reader, a licensor of a trade secret license should seek an explicit acknowledgment that, despite disclosure to the licensee, the licensed material (trade secret and know-how) remains the sole property of the licensor and that all use thereof will cease upon expiration or termination of the license.

While the loss of secrecy may (actually, should) result in termination of a trade secret license, it should not be assumed that a licensee must pay royalties until such an event occurs. In those instances where the subject secret is susceptible to reverse engineering, a potential licensee has two choices: (1) take a license and pay a royalty; or (2) reverse engineer the secret and pay no royalties. The existence of these choices serves to put a ceiling on the royalties a prospective licensee would be willing to pay. Indeed, some trade secret licenses provide that royalties will be paid only in respect of use made during a period corresponding to the time that would have been required to reverse engineer the licensed trade secret.

Miscellaneous

As discussed in Chapter 5, a patent licensee may request warranties that use of the technology covered by the licensed patents will be free of any claim of infringement by any third party. A similar request may be made by the licensee of trade secrets and know-how. Such a request is unreasonable in the context of a patent license, and is equally unreasonable in the context of a license of trade secrets and know-how. The only appropriate warranty to be made by the licensor is that the licensor has the right and authority to grant the license and that the grant of the license would not constitute a violation of any agreement between the licensor and any third party.

Just as in patent licenses, the question of rights to improvements may arise in the context of trade secret and know-how licenses. Licensees, of course, wish to include all such improvements in the existing license— at no additional cost—while licensors generally seek further compensation. The answer to the question is generally about the same as in patent licenses (see Chapter 5 for a more complete discussion of this issue). Also, just as in patent licenses, indemnification and insurance for any product liability claims should be required of the licensee.

Your Place or Mine?

While patents and copyrights are governed by federal law, the law relating to trade secrets is state law. There is a surprising degree of variability among the states, both in the statutes relating to trade secrets and in the case decisions interpreting these statutes. Where the licensor and licensee are in different states, a question arises as to which state's laws should govern the license (this is known to lawyers as a "choice of laws" question). Given the substantial differences that exist, this is not a question to be taken lightly, but should be referred to a knowledgeable professional.

Summary

Trade secrets and know-how can take a wide variety of forms, and a license on such property must define very clearly what is being licensed. The licensee may seek sufficient assistance from the licensor to enable it to utilize the licensed property effectively; the licensor, however, should take care not to include anything in the license that could be construed as a warranty of the suitability or effectiveness of the licensed property.

Know-how and trade secret licenses are global in scope, and they may have a limited term or may continue for as long as the licensee continues to utilize the licensed property. If the secret becomes publicly known and the license provides for the termination of the license in such an event, the licensee may invoke this provision to terminate the license and continue to use the information without paying any royalties; if the license does not include such a provision, the licensee may be compelled to pay royalties for using information that is now public knowledge.

Licenses of trade secrets and know-how should include provisions for the maintenance of secrecy. In both the licensee's and licensor's companies, only those employees with a "need to know" should be allowed access to confidential or proprietary information. For this reason, the obligation to maintain confidentiality should survive the termination of a license.

If the license includes a provision for termination in the event that the licensed information becomes publicly known, the licensor must be sure to qualify the term "publicly known." Otherwise, an unscrupulous licensee may attempt to reconstruct the information from publicly available sources in order to terminate the license and enjoy the intellectual property royalty-free.

A licensor should not warrant that the licensed trade secret or know-how is free of any claim of infringement by a third party, only that the licensor has the right and authority to grant the license.

CHAPTER 7

Trademark Licenses

After reading this chapter you will be able to

- Understand what rights to the use of a mark are granted by a trademark license and what limits the licensor may place on that use

- Recognize how the use of a well-known trademark can help a licensee's sales and how the licensee's misuse of the mark can harm the licensor

- Recognize the consequences stemming from a "naked license"

- Determine how a licensor can ensure that the licensee will maintain high standards of quality in the products on which the mark appears

- Understand what is meant by "blurring" of a mark

- Understand how a company should use its *own* mark correctly to avoid losing it

- Understand what should be done with inventory of goods bearing a licensed trademark after the termination of the license (and what *not* to allow your licensee to do)

- Determine who bears responsibility if a consumer is injured by a product bearing a licensed mark

- Understand how trademark and service mark licensing relates to franchising

Licenses of patents and trade secrets merely allow the licensee to share the licensor's technology; a trademark license allows the licensee to share the licensor's *good name*. It is the licensor's efforts to preserve and protect the licensed marks that distinguish the trademark license.

Definitions

When licensing patents or trade secrets, the definition of Licensed Products is, to a certain extent, limited by the nature of the underlying technologies—as a practical matter, a particular technology can be used only to produce certain goods or services. There is no such inherent limitation on the use of a licensed trademark or service mark. As a result, it sometimes is believed that a mark in use with respect to one set of goods or services may be licensed for use in respect of any other goods or services. *Wrong.* The possessor of a mark does not necessarily have rights to all possible uses of the mark. Indeed, the right of exclusive use (or even the right to use at all) may be limited to the owner's current use. Therefore, the parties to a trademark or service mark license should verify that the licensee's proposed use (1) is within the scope of goods and services described in the trademark registration, and (2) will not infringe the rights of any third party. Similarly, where the proposed use of a mark by a licensee differs markedly from the prior use of that mark by the licensor—that is, the mark will be used by the licensee in respect of goods and services vastly different from those of the licensor—the licensor may lack a protectable right with respect to the proposed use. In such case—and in the absence of any agreement between the parties—the rights to the mark, as used in respect of the licensee's goods or services, could accrue to the first user. Rights to use the mark would belong to the new user and not the original owner. The (soon-to-be-former) licensee could then turn the tables on the (soon-to-be-former) licensor by canceling the license and using the mark without restriction.

To avoid such a development, trademark licenses commonly provide (if the licensor is alert) that all use of the licensed mark shall inure (lawyer-speak for "accrue") to the benefit of the licensor, and the licensee shall itself have no rights in the mark.

It often is believed (correctly) that the cachet of a famous trademark will stimulate the sale of otherwise pedestrian goods. Recognizing this fact of merchandising life, manufacturers of such indispensable items as baseball caps, belt buckles, T-shirts, bar glasses, bumper stickers, and travel mugs constantly beseech the owners of well-known marks for the right to prominently emblazon these marks on their goods. Recognizing an opportunity when they see one, owners of famous marks are increasingly willing to grant such licenses. The trademark owners justify this pandering on the grounds that it will increase the exposure of the mark in the marketplace and broaden the range of goods in respect of which the mark is protected.

While there is, in fact, some (little) validity to these arguments, the real (obvious) reason for such licensing is money—the purveyors of this dreadful dreck will collectively pay substantial royalties for the use of the licensed marks. In order to maximize their licensing revenues, the trademark owners tend to define the permitted field of use quite narrowly, thus subdividing the spectrum of licensed crap (known to the licensors as "promotional" or "ancillary" goods) into as many segments as possible, each of which potentially may be licensed on an exclusive (higher royalty rate, guaranteed annual minimum royalty) basis.

Quality Control

Naked License: Not as Much Fun as It Sounds

It is a function of a trademark or service mark to serve as a standard of quality. A consumer is entitled to assume, for example, that a product bearing a trademark is of the same quality as other goods bearing the same mark. Thus, trademarks and service marks perform a public service as well as a more obvious marketing function. Clearly, it is in the best interest of the owner of a mark to have it associated with high standards of quality. If a mark is licensed, it is in the best interest of the licensor for the licensee to maintain those high-quality standards.

As if self-interest were not enough, the law actually *requires* that a licensor take steps to ensure that the goods or services of a licensee meet the quality standards (it is hoped) previously established by the licensor. Until the early part of the twentieth century, trademarks were considered solely as an indicator of origin—they served merely to identify, to the public, the source of the goods on which they appeared. Use of a mark by anyone other than its owner would, therefore, mislead the public as to the true origin of the goods bearing the mark. For this reason, the licensing of trademarks was prohibited. During the 1930s, however, trademark doctrine evolved from "source theory" to "quality theory." Under this new theory, trademarks served not only as an indicator of source, but also as an indicator of *quality*. The public could assume that every item bearing a given mark was of the same quality as every other item bearing the same mark. Under this theory, if a trademark licensee maintained the same quality standards as the trademark owner, no fraud would be worked on the public by use of the mark by one other than its owner.

 TIPS & TECHNIQUES

An assignment of a trademark, without an assignment of the corresponding goodwill—known as an assignment in gross or a naked assignment—will invalidate rights to the subject mark.

In order to provide a licensor of a mark with a basis to enforce this obligation, trademark and service mark licenses *must* include a quality control provision. A license that lacks such a provision is known as a naked license. The grant of such a naked license may result in the licensor's loss of proprietary rights in the licensed mark. Although the specific language may, of course, vary, quality control provisions broadly require the licensee to maintain "high" quality standards; to comply with all applicable laws, regulations, and industry standards; and to refrain from any act or practice that would tarnish the reputation of the licensed mark. (Technically, the requirement is not that a licensee maintains *high* quality standards, merely that the licensee maintains the quality standards of the licensor; however, few licensors care to admit that their quality is anything but "high.") Where the licensed mark is to be applied to goods for which samples or prototypes are in existence, the quality control provision may simply require that all licensed goods be of the same quality as the sample. The licensor also may insist on approval rights with respect to the design and execution of any new product to be sold under the licensed mark. Mere inclusion of the appropriate quality control provisions in a license is not enough. The licensor actually must *enforce* the provisions.

Trademark Usage

Preserving Your Good Name

A tool that is misused may be dulled or broken. A trademark or service mark that is misused may be blurred or lost. Blurring of a mark occurs when a mark is used in varied or altered forms. Failure to present a mark in a single, consistent manner causes the consumer's perception of the mark to become uncertain or blurred, with a resultant loss of distinctiveness and recognition—a slow deterioration of the mark.

If a mark becomes the generic term for the goods or services in respect of which it is used, it ceases to be protectable and becomes freely available for use by any and all who so desire. Such a loss may result from the near-universal practice of copywriters and marketing managers to misuse marks—using them as nouns or verbs (in case the reader has forgotten, a trademark is an adjective). To combat this suicidal tendency, the licensor of a mark should insist on the right of prior approval of all packaging, advertising, and any other instance of usage of the licensed mark. Although not explicitly stated in the typical license, approval should include verification that any federally registered marks are properly identified as such.

Because of the immediate and irreparable damage that may ensue from a licensee's failure to adhere to quality standards or from a licensee's misuse of licensed marks (actually because of the glacial speed of infringement litigation proceedings), it is advisable—and common practice—for the parties to stipulate, in a trademark or service mark license, to the prompt entry of appropriate preliminary and permanent injunctions terminating such activities.

As noted in Chapter 5, recovery of damages for patent infringement is greatly facilitated if products are marked with patent numbers. A somewhat similar rule applies to the use of the ® symbol in conjunction with registered trademarks or service marks. Although few, if any, licensees object to such use, it behooves the licensor to see that it is not overlooked.

Termination

Left Holding the Bag

A trademark or service mark license may end because it came to the end of its term or because it was terminated. Termination is virtually always the result of a material breach of the license by the licensee. What is to become of any inventory of goods bearing the licensed mark when termination occurs? In general, the appropriate answer depends on the reason for the termination. If the termination was occasioned by the licensee's failure to maintain proper quality, the licensor obviously should not allow sale of the inventory. Similarly, a licensee should not be permitted to utilize any packaging bearing improper trademark usage.

In other cases, a licensee may be allowed a reasonable period of time to dispose of existing inventory. Such permission, however, should apply only to inventory kept in the ordinary course of business. This limitation is intended to forestall the tactics of certain licensees of questionable ethics and uncertain parentage that build up inventory in anticipation of termination.

Somewhat counterintuitively, it also may be desirable to prevent a terminated licensee from dumping inventory at distress or unusually low prices, as this will adversely affect sales of other licensees and also may tarnish the licensed mark. Thus, permission should extend only to sales made at regular or preexisting price levels. In any event, it should be stated explicitly (generally in the section of the license devoted to calculation and payment of royalties) that royalties accrue on all sales made after the term or termination of the license, and that the licensee's obligation to pay accrued royalties is continuing in nature and survives termination of the license.

TIPS & TECHNIQUES

Typically, trademark licenses have terms of one (1) to five (5) years. Nonexclusive trademark licenses typically bear royalty rates of 3 to 7 percent.

Indemnification

Consider a licensed product manufactured to standards set by the licensor, perhaps in accord with a design approved by the licensor. When sold, it bore the licensor's mark. A consumer injured by a licensed product may assert (sometimes truthfully) that the product was purchased in reliance on the licensor's good name and reputation and/or duty of supervision and quality control. Whatever the rationale employed by the (allegedly) injured consumer—or, more accurately, the consumer's attorney—the fact of the matter is that the licensor almost always has a deeper pocket than does the licensee. Thus, it is highly likely that the trademark licensor will be a defendant in any product liability suit involving a licensed product. Proper indemnification is, therefore, extremely important. Indemnification, however, is worth no more than the indemnitor. The most carefully worded provision, reinforced by the best of intentions and goodwill, is still worth no more than the assets that back it. The prudent licensor also will require, from all but the most financially secure licensees, the provision of a suitable policy of product liability insurance, naming the licensor as an additional insured party.

Enforcement

Because a trademark is imbued with public purpose—identification of source and indication of quality—the failure to enforce trademark rights is deemed, by the courts, to be an unacceptable breach of the owner's duty. As a result, failure to police (lawyerspeak for "watch for unauthorized use of") a mark and to take action against infringers is held to constitute abandonment of the mark.

To prevent such a loss, a trademark owner should, obviously, *police the mark and take action against infringers.* When a mark is licensed, the matter becomes somewhat more complex. Trademarks are similar to patents in that standing to sue for infringement rests with the owner of the mark (or, in the case of a patent, the owner of the patent), unless an exclusive license has been granted that conveys to the licensee "substantially all the indicia of ownership." (This excludes licenses that, for example, are limited as to territory or to less than all goods covered by the licensed mark.) If such a license has been granted, it is the licensee that has standing to sue. A licensor, when granting an exclusive license, should provide for enforcement of the licensed mark(s) by the licensee. At a minimum, the license should provide that the licensee will join with the owner (at the owner's expense) to take action against infringers.

A Couple of Parting Words

Trademark and service mark licensing can blend almost imperceptibly into franchising. Franchising, essentially, combines a trademark or service mark license with the provision of marketing or promotional assistance, controls over the business or manufacturing methods employed by the franchisee, and the payment of both initial fees and running royalties. Franchises are subject to regulation by the Federal Trade Commission (FTC) as well as 15 states, at least one of which (New York) imposes criminal sanctions for violations. If a proposed license exhibits—or might possibly exhibit—these (franchising) characteristics, seek legal counsel before proceeding.

In addition to concerns about possible franchising, trademark licensing may give rise to questions of possible violation of the antitrust laws, in particular the Sherman Act. Antitrust issues primarily arise when multiple trademark licenses are granted, each limited to a specific geographic area (possible "horizontal market division"). Before embarking on a campaign of fancy trademark licensing, consult a professional.

Summary

Having the right to use a trademark on one product does not imply free rein to use the mark on other products. A licensor should make certain that a licensee's proposed use will not infringe the rights of a third party; in order to protect the licensor itself, trademark licenses commonly provide that all use of the licensed mark shall inure to the benefit of the licensor.

Trademarks and service marks serve as indicators of quality, which means that a well-known and respected mark lends credibility to the licensee—and that credibility can be lost or tarnished if the licensee does not uphold the high standard of quality for which the mark is known. By law, trademark and service mark licenses, therefore, must include a quality control provision; a license without such a provision is called a "naked license."

A mark is "blurred" when it is used in varied or altered forms, and this misuse can result in deterioration of the mark. Trademarks always must be used as adjectives; using them as nouns or verbs is an example of misuse that can lead to the mark becoming generic and, therefore, lost. The licensor should insist on the right to prior approval of all uses of the mark and also should make sure that its own copywriters and advertising department are using the mark correctly.

If a trademark or service mark license is terminated because of the licensee's failure to maintain proper quality, the licensor should not allow the remaining marked inventory to be sold, which would further damage the mark. If the license simply reaches the end of its term, the licensee should be allowed to sell the remaining inventory—but not at deeply discounted prices that could tarnish the mark and adversely affect sales of licensed products by other licensees.

Proper indemnification protects the licensor from any suits brought by consumers who are injured by a licensed product, and is, thus, very important. However, any indemnification provision should be backed up by sufficient assets to reinforce it. Licensors should insist on a provision for a product liability insurance policy.

Since trademark and service mark licensing can strongly resemble franchising, competent legal counsel should be sought when any such license is proposed.

CHAPTER 8

Copyright Licenses

After reading this chapter you will be able to

- Understand how copyright law protects software and how software licenses work

- Understand the responsibility of the licensor in the event that licensed software fails

- Identify the issues involved in licensing automated databases

- Understand what a company should know before it attempts to reuse a successful ad campaign

I t is not an idea but merely a particular expression of the idea that is protected by copyright. A copyright license typically affords the licensee the right to reproduce and distribute (lawyerspeak for "sell") copies of the expression. Thus, in the popular mind, copyright licensing is associated with book publishing, music recording, and movies. Such licensing is highly specialized and of interest only to the relatively few persons employed (even including gofers, hangers-on, and wannabes, the number is low) in those industries. For the businessperson, the most significant instances of copyright licensing pertain to computer software and advertising and promotional materials.

Computer Software Licenses

Shrinking Opportunities

Other than rabbits, nothing is so readily reproduced as computer software. Three decades ago, software companies were faced with the problem of widespread piracy of computer programs. Once a copy of a program was sold, the buyer was free to rent it to others who might (unless they were either incredibly ethical or stupid) reproduce it before returning the rented copy. Such copying was, of course, an infringement of any copyright in the software, but, hey, this was the 1970s —free expression, free love, free software; besides, it was uneconomical and impractical for the software companies to pursue individual infringers, and, therefore, such enforcement was nonexistent.

Rising to the challenge, the companies opted to license the software rather than sell it. While they lost control over a unit of software if they sold it, they could maintain their control if they licensed it. A suitable (to the software company) license was packaged with the software. A notice on the package warns that breaking of the shrink-wrapped seal shall be deemed an acceptance of the license by the consumer (hence the term "shrink-wrap license"). Software downloaded from the Internet is similarly subject to a license that consumers accept when they click their mouse. (This license is known, not surprisingly, as a click-wrap license.)

What if, however, there is an opportunity to negotiate a software license, rather than being forced to accept one prepared by a software megamonster? Four issues are paramount:

1. The scope of use

2. Performance guarantees

3. Termination provisions

4. Indemnification

The purpose of software licenses is to increase the sales (technically, the license royalties) of the subject software. Basically, this is accomplished by so limiting the use of a licensed program that the licensee is induced—if not to say compelled—to license additional or multiple copies (and pay additional royalties) in order to satisfy all its needs. Thus, the grant clause is highly specific as to the intended use, the place of use, and, most important, the number of users. If the license permits installation of the licensed software on a computer network, the maximum number of network users typically is specified. The license fee or royalty generally is dependent on this number.

Often, licensed software is critical to the operation of the licensee's business. In such cases, loss of the right to use the software, as might result from the sudden and unexpected termination of the license, could be catastrophic. To avoid such a disaster, many licensees seek termination provisions that allow a grace period, during which time they can scramble desperately for alternate software or beg shamelessly to have their license reinstated. In exchange for such a munificent gesture, licensors typically demand audit provisions—to facilitate the detection of any violation of license restrictions—and rather severe liquidated damages (stipulated penalties for breach of contract).

Because licensed software may be critical to the operation of the licensee's business, a failure of that software may result in significant damages (lawyerspeak for a claim for "a whole lot o' money"). Licensors, of course, do everything in their power to limit, if not eliminate, their exposure in such events. A disclaimer of all damages would, most likely, be deemed unconscionable and, therefore, unenforceable. (If this doesn't sound familiar, the reader should revisit Chapter 2.) The fallback position licensors adopt most often is to exclude consequential damages (the damages that really matter) and limit a licensee's recovery to the amount paid in royalties or license fees. Often, licensors will try to limit their responsibility with respect to the performance of the licensed software by disclaiming any warranties that it is fit for any particular purpose. If these warranties are disclaimed (which, by the way, must be done exactly according to the dictates of the Uniform Commercial Code [UCC]), the software need only be "of merchantable quality," that is, not total crap. Licensees of custom or customized software, who really are seeking software adapted to a particular purpose, should pay particular attention to the warranty provisions of their licenses. They should, in addition, ensure that the license clearly specifies the performance criteria for the licensed software, and that the licensor warrants that the licensed software will meet these criteria.

While knowledgeable licensors of patents and trade secrets do not warrant their licensees freedom from third-party claims of infringement, the practice followed by software licensors is different. Licensors of standard (not custom or customized) software typically warrant freedom from such claims. However, not all warranties are equal. Possible remedies, by the licensor, in the event that the licensed software is found to infringe the rights of a third party, may include:

- Providing a license from the third party at no cost to the licensee (excellent)

- Providing substitute software free of any such claims (probably acceptable, but may involve some disruption during changeover)

- Return of the license fees (probably unacceptable, as it may result in severe business interruption)

- Read all warranties carefully.

Finally, copyright law allows the purchaser of a copyrighted computer program, as a matter of right, to make a single archival or backup copy. Licensees, however, have no such right unless it is granted to them in their license. A prudent licensee will insist on such a license provision.

Postscript

Following the 1990 revision of the copyright law, a purchaser of copyrighted software is prohibited from renting it to others. Despite this change, the practice of shrink-wrap licensing continues.

Automated Databases

An automated database is a collection of data arranged in an organized format so as to be suitable for use in a computer. Automated databases may be protected by copyright if they embody sufficient creativity in the selection and arrangement of the data. Simple transfer of data from books or paper to a computer hard drive will not yield a protectable database, nor, at present, will the mere expenditure of great effort suffice. The use of an automated database may be licensed, with fees based on extent of use or simply on a monthly or annual basis. Typically, access to the database is controlled through the use of passwords.

Potential licensees generally are most concerned with the frequency with which the database is updated. Licensors generally are most concerned with disclaiming any liability for any loss that may in any way relate to any use of the data which may in any way prove to be in any way less than completely accurate. (The authors trust that the reader gets the message.)

Advertising and Promotional Materials

That Was Great; Let's Do It Again

Often an organization will commission a photographer, commercial artist, copywriter, or a combination of such individuals to create an advertising or promotional piece, intending that it be used only once or only in some other limited manner. Then, finding the piece to be unexpectedly successful, or simply through sloth and greed (they're lazy and cheap), the piece, or portions thereof, is reused. Often, such an organization is sued for copyright infringement. What happened?

The organization failed to secure an assignment of copyrights from the creator(s) of the work it has so blithely reproduced. Because the individuals in question were not employees, there is a substantial probability that the works they created were not works for hire (see Chapter 3), and the copyrights to these works vested in the authors, not the organization that retained them. The organization's reuse of the works constituted an unauthorized reproduction and distribution of the copyrighted works (and, possibly, the unauthorized creation of a derivative work)—in other words, copyright infringement.

An alert (euphemism for "not brain-dead") organization might avoid problems of this sort by securing an assignment of all copyrights from any consultants it might retain. Such assignments are, however, in disfavor with the "artists" for the obvious reason that they reduce income (no residuals). The artists prefer to license their works. Therefore, if assignment is refused, an option to renew or extend the proferred license should be secured. In any event, it is wise to verify the legal status of artwork and advertising or promotional copy before recycling it.

Summary

Copyrights do not protect ideas but expressions of those ideas. For most businesspeople, the most significant instances of copyright licensing pertain to software and advertising and promotional materials.

The individual software user automatically enters into a license with the software manufacturer by breaking the seal on the software package, also known as shrink-wrap licensing. The advent of downloadable software programs brought us the "click-wrap" license, in which the consumer must accept the terms with a click of the mouse in order to download the software.

Businesses with multiple users often negotiate a different kind of software license, one that is specific to the intended use, place of use, and number of users. A license permitting the installation of the software on the company's network will specify the maximum number of users to be allowed to access the program.

Licensees of business software should ensure that the termination provisions of the license include a grace period and also should pay special attention to the warranty provisions for the licensor's responsibility should the software fail.

Automated databases may be protected by copyright if sufficient creativity has been used in the selection and arrangement of their data. The use of an automated database may be licensed based on extent of use or on a monthly or annual basis.

Before reproducing any ad or promotional campaign, a company should be sure that it has the right to do so. Without an assignment of copyright, the works may well still belong to the artists who created them, not the organization that commissioned the work.

CHAPTER 9

Royalties and Royalty Rates

After reading this chapter you will be able to

- Identify the difference between a "paid-up" license and a "running royalty" license

- Understand what factors enter into royalty rate determination

- Understand the importance of risk reduction in offering a carrot license and which "extras" may sweeten the pot for the prospective licensee

The key issue in any licensing transaction, the one generally considered first and longest, is the royalty. How much should the licensee pay the licensor for the right to use the licensed property? A related issue is the form the license royalty is to take, either a paid-up or a running royalty.

Paid-up Licenses

A "paid-up" license is one wherein the royalty is a fixed sum. It may be paid in a lump sum or over a period of time in accordance with an agreed-on payment schedule. Once agreed on, the sum is independent of the future success of the licensee. Sales by the licensee may prove high or collapse to virtually nil, but the royalty remains fixed at the agreed sum. This is not to say that the paid-up royalty is not determined on the basis of future sales. Quite the contrary, a critical step in the determination of a paid-up royalty is the agreement by the licensor and the licensee upon a forecast of future licensed sales. Obviously, the greater the anticipated sales, the higher the royalty that will be demanded by the licensor and the greater the amount that the licensee will be willing to pay. Therein lies the rub. Sales forecasting is difficult under the best of circumstances. It is much more difficult when self-interest is involved. Paid-up licenses thus are best suited to those situations where future sales are relatively predictable. Since the difficulty of forecasting is generally proportional to the length of the forecast period, it follows that forecasts for short periods are more confidently made and are more likely to be agreed to by the parties. Thus, paid-up licenses are found more frequently where the license term is short, either because the licensee desires only a limited term or because the licensed properties (patents) will expire shortly.

Paid-up licenses are strongly preferred by large companies, which seek to avoid the inconvenience of accounting for sales of licensed products and of processing the periodic royalty payments inherent in a running royalty license. Strangely, paid-up licenses also are generally preferred by small licensors. A small licensor often has only one patent (or a few related patents) to license. If any harm should befall the patent—such as a judicial finding of invalidity, unenforceability, or noninfringement—the licensor is left without income. Royalties in paid-up licenses are, unless otherwise agreed, nonrefundable. Thus, small licensors may reduce their risk through the use of paid-up licensing. Where the licensee is a start-up company, temporarily flush as a result of venture capital financing, a licensor might well prefer to grant a paid-up license—getting the royalties while the opportunity presents, before the funds are frittered away.

Running Royalty Licenses

One way to avoid or minimize disagreements as to future sales is to base the royalty on actual sales. If the license provides for a royalty based on actual sales of the licensed product(s)—a "running royalty"—the need to forecast future sales volumes and prices is obviated. "It is what it is," and the patent owner gets an agreed percentage of it, generally payable quarterly. Of course, this still begs the question of how to set the royalty rate. Obviously, a running royalty would be preferred by a licensee with cash flow problems. Also, where a license pertains to industrial as opposed to consumer products, some licensees believe that the existence of a running royalty facilitates passing the cost along to their customers.

Royalty Rate Determination

In essence, the royalty effects a sharing of the benefits enjoyed by the licensee by reason of the license. Thus, ideally (!), the royalty rate is set at one-quarter to one-half of the expected benefit or anticipated operating profit (gross, not net) of the licensee. This is sometimes known as the 25 percent rule. If, for example, this rule was applied in a situation where the licensee anticipates a gross operating profit of 16 percent of the sale price of a patented product, the royalty rate would be 4 percent (16% x .25).

 IN THE REAL WORLD

Determining Royalty Rates

On the question of patent license royalty rates, the leading case is *Georgia-Pacific Corp. v. United States Plywood Corp.*, 318 F. Supp. 1116 [S.D.N.Y. 1970], which lists 15 factors to be considered when determining a rate.

When seeking agreement as to the division of these profits, the licensor typically points to the investment required to create the licensed property as justification for a higher royalty. The licensee typically retorts that such investment is a "sunk cost" (economist's term meaning "irrelevant historical data"). The licensee then points to the risks it must accept and the investment it must make before any profit can be realized, as support for a lower royalty. From an economic viewpoint, this latter argument should be more persuasive.

Various other factors also may enter into the royalty negotiation. For example, if use of the licensed property somehow will stimulate sales of other products or services of the licensee, a higher royalty would be justified. The importance of the licensed property to the product or service in which it is incorporated should be considered, as should the availability and general acceptability of substitutes for the licensed properties. Obviously, the more significant the licensed property as a component of the product in which it is incorporated, the higher the royalty it can command. Similarly, a property for which there are few or no available substitutes—or for which the substitutes are unacceptably costly—can command a higher royalty than a property for which alternatives abound.

As usual, real life is not as simple as theory (see Exhibit 9.1, "Ingredients of a Royalty Rate"). Either or both of the parties may seek to support their positions by reference to the royalty rates of other existing licenses, the implicit assumption being that the rates in these other licenses are somehow relevant to the question of the appropriate rate for the license at issue. Thus, for example, in patent licensing, licensors generally will point to the royalty rates in licenses they had previously granted under the same patents. This, in fact, is relevant. Either party may argue about "typical" or "standard in the industry" rates. This argument is relevant only if the patent licenses used for comparison are, in fact, comparable to the one under consideration. Licensees occasionally may point to the royalty rates in other licenses they have taken or licenses they have granted. Again, this is relevant only if the properties that are the subject of these other licenses are comparable to the property that is the subject of the license being negotiated. (See Appendix B for industry royalty rates.)

EXHIBIT 9.1

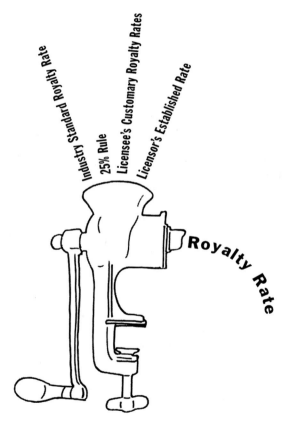

Ingredients of a Royalty Rate

Industry Standard Royalty Rate

25% Rule

Licensee's Customary Royalty Rates

Licensor's Established Rate

Royalty Rate

"Laws are like sausages. It's better not to see them being made."

—Otto von Bismarck

As noted in Chapter 4, exclusive licenses generally bear a higher royalty than would a nonexclusive license of the same property. Where an exclusive license is of the running royalty type, it is quite common to include a provision requiring the payment of specified "guaranteed" or "minimum" royalties even if such amount would not otherwise be due. Such requirements are considered part of the premium paid by the licensee for exclusivity. In a variation of this requirement, failure of the licensee to meet specified royalty levels results in a conversion of the license from an exclusive one to a nonexclusive one.

TIPS & TECHNIQUES

Resources available on the Internet and in royalty rate publications (not to mention consultants who make their living by advising on the appropriate royalty rates) may be useful in finding comparable licensing transactions.

The 15-Step Program

What happens, in the case of an allegedly infringed patent, if the parties are unable to reach agreement as to a reasonable royalty? Litigation. The question is taken out of the hands of the parties and placed before a judge—in a bench trial—or a jury. In either event, the standard applied to determine the appropriate royalty rate is the same: the 15 factors set forth in the seminal case *Georgia-Pacific Corp. v. United States Plywood Corp.* (See the factors listed in Appendix J.) Many of these factors are rather nebulous, meaning that the parties, who were unable to agree on a single issue, will be compelled to argue—in court (hence, at great expense)—about 15 issues. Often, one or more of the factors may be inapplicable.

Nevertheless, parties seeking to settle allegations of patent infringement, but who believe they have reached an impasse in license negotiations, should carefully consider the costs of litigation before turning to the courts. Moreover, as a general rule, royalty rates determined by a court are higher than rates freely negotiated by the parties, which rates are deemed, by the courts, to have been implicitly discounted for the uncertainties encountered at litigation.

TIPS & TECHNIQUES

If you have no clue what royalty rate to ask (or offer), a 5 percent royalty rate is a good place to start. Statistically, most royalty rates tend to cluster around this number.

IN THE REAL WORLD

Don't Get Taken: Know What It's Worth

An inventor, when asked what he wanted for a license under his patent, admitted that he never was able to afford an engagement ring for his wife. He offered to accept $20,000, with which he could purchase a diamond ring, plus a 1 percent running royalty. The prospective licensee, which happened to be a large multinational concern, offered to double the amount of the up-front royalty payment in lieu of the running royalty. The deal was closed for $40,000, when, in fact, the inventor could have gotten much, much more. The moral of the story: Do your homework, learn what the licensed property is worth, and don't get blinded by the sight of a pile of cash.

Risk and Price—Package Deals in Intellectual Property Licensing

Businesspeople as a rule prefer to avoid or minimize risk. Given a choice, they gravitate toward those investments or projects that involve the least uncertainty at any given rate of return. Obviously, the prospect of a large reward may tempt people to accept risk; as between different investments offering similar potential rewards, the one perceived as presenting the least risk will be the most popular and, hence, will command the highest price. This principle lies at the heart of the franchising industry.

Franchise purchasers pay a substantial premium over the costs they would otherwise incur in starting a similar business *ab initio* (the Latin is so much more impressive than the corresponding "from scratch"). What does the franchise purchaser receive in exchange for this premium? Greater certainty—as much as anything can be certain in business. The franchisee receives detailed specifications, formulas, and process directions for the products or services that the new business will offer. Lists of suppliers also are provided, as is training for employees. All necessary equipment and tools arrive in a package. Frequently, the franchisor includes assistance with such things as site selection, application for necessary permits and approvals, and establishing accounting and other control systems. Moreover, and most important, the franchise includes a license under the franchisor's trademarks.

The same principle applies to intellectual property licensing. It is most certainly possible to assign or license a patent, for example, without offering anything more. Such transactions, however, are generally in the nature of patent enforcement actions. In these instances, a matter of patent infringement is (more or less) amicably resolved when the infringer acquires the infringed patent, or a license thereunder (so-called stick licensing—see Chapter 4). Such a license engenders little technological risk—the infringing product is already on the market. Indeed, by taking a license, the former infringer actually reduces its risk by eliminating the risk of being sued for patent infringement.

Quite a different situation results, however, when a party is not already using the patented technology. In such a case, the party is under no compulsion to acquire the patent or take a license. Adoption of a new—and, therefore, untested and unproven—technology presents substantial risks. The technology may prove to be flawed. It may require further (expensive) development before it is ready for the market. Even if there are no technological problems, or if such problems are solved successfully, the technology still may fail in the market for any of a variety of reasons. The greater the perceived risk associated with a new technology, the greater the reluctance to invest substantial resources to acquire and commercialize it and, as a result, the lower the price the technology will be able to command. Once this relationship between price and risk is recognized, the solution becomes obvious: Reduce the risk associated with a technology, and the price it commands will increase.

Risk reduction is, in essence, a matter of providing solutions to those problems that would otherwise constitute risks. Just as a franchisee willingly pays a premium for a "turnkey" business operation, so too will a prospective assignee or licensee pay a premium for a market-ready or market-proven technology. In other words, a tested and proven new product or service, covered by a patent, will fetch a much higher price than the patent alone. Therefore, whenever possible, sell a product, not a patent. Package the patent with applicable trademarks, design specifications, blueprints, test results, process know-how, quality assurance procedures, lists of qualified suppliers, market research data, and anything else that will facilitate commercialization of the patented technology. Such information is of value to a prospective buyer in two respects: It reduces the additional investment required to achieve commercialization, and it reduces the risk of failure. It is comparatively easy to sell a successful product or service. The closer an invention is to market—the fewer the remaining problems—the more it will bring. Moreover, a package license, including trademarks and know-how, may continue generating royalties after the patents in the package have expired.

Summary

A paid-up license is one with a fixed-sum royalty, while the royalty in a "running royalty" license is based on actual ongoing sales. A reasonable royalty rate often is set at 25 percent of the expected operating profit of the licensee. When in doubt, a royalty rate of 5 percent is generally a good opening position.

One factor used in determining the royalty rate for a new license is the royalty rates of existing licenses of the same patents. Another factor is "typical" industry rates for comparable inventions.

When offering a license on a new technology, the prospective licensor should seek to minimize the risk involved with that technology by offering a "package deal" to help market the invention. Although the invention still may fail for a variety of reasons, the appearance of risk is minimized by making the technology as market-ready as possible. Information, such as know-how, design specifications, applicable trademarks, and so on, serves to reduce the effort and investment needed to bring the product to market.

CHAPTER 10

Policing and Enforcement of Licenses

After reading this chapter you will be able to

- Use practical tips for ensuring that a licensee makes royalty payments on a timely basis—and that the sales report is accurate

- Understand how a licensee can be sure that the licensor meets all of its license obligations

- Understand how a licensee can work with other licensees to make sure that it is paying the lowest royalty rate possible

- Understand why a licensee should verify that the licensor is maintaining the licensed patents

From the Viewpoint of the Licensor

It Ain't Over Till It's Over

Many licensors believe that the battle is over when a license is finally executed. *Wrong!* After a license is executed, it must be policed. First and foremost, is the licensee timely making all royalty payments required under the license agreement? Note that the foregoing is a compound question (lawyerspeak for "tricky"); let's parse it:

- Timely: Was payment received within the allotted time?
- All: Were all sales covered by the license reported?
- Made: Were all required payments actually received?

A surprising number of licensees file away (and forget) their executed licenses without docketing scheduled payments. *Do not do this.* Some licensees, for example, "forget" to make their quarterly royalty payments. It is up to the licensor to provide a written reminder when a payment is overdue. This, of course, requires that the licensor knows when a payment is overdue.

Not all licensees report all licensed sales (surprise!). Keep track of all licensees' payments. Does the current payment seem unusual as compared to past payments or the payments of other licensees? If a licensee claims business is poor, check the licensee's website. Is the licensee boasting to the world about how business is expanding? Are there any inconsistencies? If the licensee is a public company, peruse its 10-Q filings. What is it telling its shareholders? Check the licensee's annual reports, press releases, and other publicly available sources of information.

Monitor the licensee's product literature. (Most often, this is available on the licensee's Web site.) Are there any new products, or new models of old products, that are subject to the terms of the license but are not being reported (and for which no royalties are being paid)?

Licenses should include a provision allowing the licensor to audit the books of a licensee to the extent of verifying the accuracy of the licensee's reports of sales of licensed goods. Such audit provisions should provide that the licensee will bear the cost of an audit if a material discrepancy—usually 5 percent or more of the amount properly due—is discovered. Audits can be rather costly and. therefore, are not to be undertaken lightly. Often, however, the mere threat of an audit will produce the desired result—the licensee discovers an unfortunate error and tenders a check (sometimes with apologies, sometimes without).

Is the licensee complying with provisions that limit the scope of the license? If the license includes geographic limitations, is the licensee selling outside of the licensed market area? If the license includes technical limitations on the licensed product, such as those on size, power, capacity, and the like, verify that none of the products being sold falls within the proscribed areas.

Periodically request (in writing) verification that the licensee is complying with the various prophylactic provisions (it sounds exciting, but it's not) of the license. Are patent numbers being properly marked on products? Are proper copyright notices being placed on publications? Are licensed trademarks being used properly, and is the quality of the goods on which the licensed marks appear being properly maintained?

Finally, face the burdens of property ownership. If the licensed properties are not maintained, eventually there will be no properties to license (and, hence, no royalties). Make sure that patent maintenance fees are paid and that trademark registration renewals and affidavits of use are filed.

From the Viewpoint of the Licensee

Okay. You are working hard and diligently (albeit reluctantly) paying your royalties. You are entitled to some consideration (see Chapter 2). Remember why you took that license in the first place—you had to. The last thing you want now is to have your competitors utilizing, for free, the same properties for which you are paying so dearly, or competing in a market where you are paying royalties to secure a monopoly. If your license has an enforcement requirement, hold the licensor to it. If the licensor is unwilling or unable to meet its obligations, you may be relieved of your obligation to pay further royalties.

Is the licensor updating and increasing the body of licensed properties? Are the licensed products or technologies being improved? Are new ones being introduced? Are new editions of licensed works being created? Are these new products, new editions, or new improvements being promptly disclosed to you, the oppressed licensee slaving away under the oppressive burden of exorbitant royalties? Failure of the licensor to disclose these advances, and to include them in the license, may be a material breach of contract. Moreover, a failure to update and renew the licensed properties may result in their growing obsolescence and a gradual decrease in their value. If time passes without improvement in the licensed properties, reexamine the value of the license. Are the old, and possibly outdated, properties still worth the price (royalty rate) negotiated when they were shiny and new? This may be the time to seek renegotiation of the royalty rate if not termination of the license. (This presupposes, of course, that the license is terminable; if not, shame on you!)

Are You Paying More Than You Should?

Like taxes, no one is obligated to pay more royalties than he or she must. If your license is nonexclusive, keep watch for new licensees. Discuss matters with them. Are their royalty rates (or other terms) more favorable than those that you secured? If your license includes a "most favored nations" clause, demand similar (improved) terms from the licensor. If your license does not include such a clause, but does include

IN THE REAL WORLD

Oops!

About 60 percent of patent owners neglect to pay maintenance fees to the Patent Office, leading to patent lapse.

suitable termination provisions, it still may be possible to renegotiate royalty terms. (If your license has neither a most favored nations clause nor suitable termination provisions, shame on you!)

It behooves a licensee, before making payment of a running royalty, to verify that royalties have, in fact, accrued. Have licensed patents expired or lapsed through nonpayment of maintenance fees? Have licensed patents been the subject of litigation, where a court has found them invalid, unenforceable, or not infringed? (Because noninfringement is highly fact-specific, check this last with competent patent counsel.) Has a licensed trade secret ceased to be a secret? Is licensed technology, either patented or protected by a trade secret or a licensed trademark, still in use? No play, no pay! (Check guaranteed minimum royalty provisions before ceasing payment.)

Some licenses provide for a reduction in royalties when a licensed patent expires. Do not rely on the licensor to notify you when such expiration occurs. Docket all expiration dates. Similarly, it is good practice to verify periodically that the licensor is maintaining the licensed patents (i.e., paying the maintenance fees). Don't pay royalties in respect of expired or lapsed patents. Note that the failure of the licensor to maintain a registered trademark or service mark would not similarly affect the obligation to pay royalties, because lapse of a trademark or service mark registration does not negate the licensor's corresponding common law rights.

Summary

After the execution of a license, the licensor must ensure that the licensee makes accurate and timely royalty payments. Whenever the licensee makes a royalty payment, the licensor should compare the current sales figure both with previous sales figures and with any publicly available information. The licensor also should periodically check the licensee's product literature and Web site to determine whether there are any new products that should be included in the license. Among the licensor's other responsibilities are maintaining the licensed properties and seeking verification that the licensee is complying with the provisions of the license, such as proper trademark usage and patent number marking on licensed products.

For its part, the licensee should ensure that its competitors, if they are using the same patented technology, are also licensees. The licensee also should verify that the licensor is keeping it up-to-date on the newest products, editions of licensed works, or improvements. If the license is nonexclusive, the licensee should be in communication with other licensees to confirm that they don't have more favorable terms or royalty rates. A "most favored nations" clause can help the licensee renegotiate its royalty terms if more favorable terms are granted to other licensees. To avoid paying royalties on expired or lapsed patents, a licensee should docket all expiration dates and verify that the licensed patents have been maintained.

CHAPTER 11

Negotiating the Deal

After reading this chapter you will be able to

- Identify the seven sins to avoid when negotiating
- Identify the seven rules for a successful negotiation

Negotiation is an art—the art of achieving the possible. A successful negotiation results in *each* of the parties receiving the greatest possible amount of that which it desires. Notice the emphasis on the word "each." In the popular vernacular, this is known as a "win-win" situation. If the negotiation process can be likened to the division of a pie, the most successful negotiators—those who ultimately get the most pie—are those who first cooperate and direct their efforts toward enlarging the size of the pie before they try to divide it.

The common and more traditional view of negotiation is that it is the process of getting, for oneself, as much as possible, by any means possible. The obvious problem with this approach is that it is adversarial. It pits the parties against each other. Rather than seeking to enlarge the pie, they fight over it, with the likely outcome being hungry, frustrated parties glaring at each other across a shriveled and smashed pastry.

Nevertheless, it takes more than good intentions and a spirit of cooperation to produce a successful negotiation. Moreover, platitudes aside, it still remains the object of negotiation to get the largest possible slice of the pie.

Negotiation Skills

No-Nos of Negotiations: The Seven Deadly Sins

Loss of Credibility. Nothing is as destructive of the negotiation process as the belief that the other side is lying. There is no point to negotiating with a party whose word cannot be relied on. Even if agreement is reached, it is unlikely to be fulfilled. Therefore, it goes without saying that scrupulous honesty is required. Avoid even the appearance of prevarication. If a statement, although true, is likely to be doubted or disbelieved, provide documentation or other support to allay any suspicions. Do not promise more than can be delivered. The benefits of exaggeration, if any, are fleeting, while the detriments are long-lived.

Surprises. Do not save bad news until the end of a negotiation. If there is something that is likely to be a stumbling block, get it on the table early. The earlier in the negotiation a problem is addressed, the more creative may be the efforts at its solution and the greater the likelihood that it will be solved successfully. Delay merely increases the difficulty. Moreover, a last-minute announcement may be viewed as a sign of bad faith by a party that considers itself "sandbagged."

Arguing or Threatening. If discourse degenerates into argument, break off negotiations until the parties have regained their composure. Argument inevitably leads to threats. Successful negotiations require that the parties establish and maintain at least a minimal working relationship. Such a relationship is not likely to survive in the face of threats.

Underestimating Your Opponent. Appearances can be deceiving. Do not assume your opponent is as dumb as he or she looks. For the same reason, do not try to outsmart your opponent. The effort may be unsuccessful. Moreover, if the attempt is detected, it will result in a complete loss of credibility. Most important, however, any benefit thus obtained is likely to be temporary. Sooner or later the victim will come to the realization that he or she has been duped and will try to wiggle out of the agreement or search for some way to achieve payback, or both.

Haggling. One form of negotiation, as most notably practiced in Middle Eastern bazaars, involves sellers starting too high, buyers starting too low, and then both parties haggling until exhaustion sets in. This may work in the bazaars of Morocco, but it doesn't work very well in licensing negotiations. This style of "positional bargaining" is adversarial by nature and tends to favor the party with the stronger will. The demands and offers are arbitrary and just for show. There is no mechanism or basis for bridging the gap between the parties' positions.

TIPS & TECHNIQUES

When negotiating a settlement of an alleged patent infringement, focus on royalty rates accepted in your industry rather than throwing an arbitrary rate on the table. Appendix B provides some licensing statistics.

Offers and counteroffers (a counteroffer is effectively the same thing as a demand, but it sounds nicer) should be made on a rational basis, and the rationale or formula should be conveyed with the offer. By providing a rationale for its offer, a party may avoid appearing arbitrary—even if the offer is rejected. Moreover, often the gap between the parties can be bridged by a reasonable adjustment to this underlying formula.

Negotiating against Yourself. An offer is rejected, but no counteroffer is made. Silence hangs heavy in the air. The party that made the rejected offer then fills the vacuum by making a new, lower offer, and then, if silence still prevails, perhaps another. This series of ever-lower bids can continue until bottom is reached. This is called negotiating against yourself. Whenever a party makes a new offer without having received a counteroffer, it encourages the other side to sit and wait to see how far the process will go. Do not feel compelled to break the silence.

Lack of Preparation. The most common of negotiating sins, lack of preparation, is also the most damaging, as it leads the sinner into further evil ways. A party that has not studied the facts is likely to misstate them. A party that has not planned an orderly presentation of its position is likely to deliver late, unpleasant surprises. A party that has not developed a series of rationales to support its various positions will have no choice but to engage in haggling.

Preparation includes investigation. Investigate your opponent. A party that does not know and understand its opponent's goals and objectives cannot hope to satisfy them at minimum cost.

Of equal importance, negotiation is founded on the premise that there are alternatives. If there are no alternatives, there can be no negotiation, only surrender. Never attempt to negotiate a deal without knowing the next best alternative. If negotiation does not yield at least as much as the next best alternative, politely get up and walk away.

Seven Rules for a Successful Negotiation

Goal Setting. Goals must be set before they can be achieved. They should be established *before* the negotiation begins. Typically, goals define a best-case scenario, which is an optimistic but not unreasonable target, and a worst-case scenario, which is the minimum acceptable outcome. Anything less than the worst-case scenario would, thus, be rejected.

The Next Best Alternative. When setting goals, keep the objectives of the other side in mind. Endeavor to enlarge the pie before seeking to grab the biggest piece. Determining or setting the minimum acceptable outcome, in turn, involves the identification of the next best alternative, or NBA. If the negotiation is unsuccessful, what other alternatives exist? The existence of alternatives sets a floor for the worst-case scenario. No negotiated outcome need, or should, be accepted that is less desirable than an available alternative. This principle highlights the importance of knowing what alternatives exist. Carefully research alternatives and determine the next best alternative before commencing negotiations.

Negotiation Strategy. Once a goal is set, how is it to be achieved? Not by happenstance! Develop an opening position, based on a sound rationale (generally this is closely related to the best-case scenario) and an ordered series of fallback positions, each of which is also supported by a rationale. Avoid making arbitrary offers. Development of rationales to yield the desired offers is not an easy task and not one to be undertaken in the heat of battle (negotiation). Plan ahead!

The Guest List. When planning a party, it is important to invite people who will get along well together. The same principle applies to negotiations. The first step in a negotiation is to establish a working relationship with the other side. If possible, include on your team individuals who already have relationships with known members of the opposing team. Such relationships may have arisen from social contacts or from previous negotiations (or litigations), or the individuals may have worked together for the same employer or studied together at the same school. Obviously, it is well to avoid individuals with known animus toward members of the other party's team.

Include someone with the necessary decision-making authority to settle the matter. Many parties will refuse to negotiate unless the opposing party includes such an individual. In cases where the negotiation takes the form of mediation, the mediator is likely to insist that both sides include individuals with full settlement authority.

A Rudder for the Ship. A ship without a rudder will not take its passengers and crew where they want to go. Similarly, a negotiation without an agenda will not take the parties where they want to go. An agenda will ensure that all issues are addressed and, equally important, that they are introduced in a logical order.

Typically, prospective licensors wish to focus on royalties; prospective licensees wish to explore the merits of the technology being offered; and alleged infringers wish to address issues related to patent validity and infringement.

Not only does an agenda set the order in which issues will be addressed, it helps avoid surprises (No-No #2).

Talk, Talk, Talk. No negotiation can succeed, or even progress, until the parties have established a dialogue. The sooner a dialogue is established, the sooner progress may commence. With this in mind, it is often advantageous to begin any negotiating session by addressing one or a few relatively benign matters. Doing this creates a nonconfrontational atmosphere in which a dialogue may more readily be established. It further facilitates early successes, which, in turn, engender a general feeling of goodwill and foster an expectation of further success.

 TIPS & TECHNIQUES

Often a party that is otherwise ready to litigate at the drop of a hat will negotiate a reasonable settlement if it is in the midst of a merger or other corporate restructuring, and fears that litigation may obstruct the planned reorganization.

Been There, Done That. As a negotiation progresses, it is vitally important to maintain a record of those points where agreement has been reached and those points that remain to be resolved. Often, after much negotiation, parties believe that they have reached agreement on an issue. It remains to be verified, however, that the understandings of the parties are the same. All too frequently, each party has heard only what it wanted to hear—or didn't hear what it didn't want to hear. When the parties believe that an agreement has been reached, one of the participants should state the terms thereof and secure the concurrence of the parties. If an issue is proving particularly troublesome, the parties may agree temporarily to put it aside. When this occurs, it is similarly advantageous to secure concurrence on the exact nature of the issue.

Summary

Set goals before commencing negotiations. Research alternatives, as they establish the minimum acceptable negotiated outcome. Develop a negotiating strategy before the negotiations begin. Loss of credibility is destructive of the negotiation process. Last-minute surprises are to be avoided, as is arguing with opponents or threatening them. Opponents should not be underestimated. Haggling is not an effective mode of negotiation, nor is bidding against oneself. Lack of preparation, which includes both investigation and planning, is the most common and most fatal negotiation error.

The probability of success in a negotiation is increased by including the appropriate people on the negotiating team and preparing an agenda for negotiation sessions. Establish a dialogue and seek to build on early successes. Maintain a record of what has been accomplished and assure that all parties agree with its accuracy.

Checklist of Patent License Terms

I. Preliminary Formal Provisions

A. Heading

  1. Parties

  2. Effective date of agreement

  3. Place where agreement made

B. Recitals

  1. Licensed subject matter

    a. Patents and applications

    b. Know-how

  2. General rights licensed

  3. Warranties

  4. Definition of terms

  5. Background of agreement

    a. Prior relationship between parties

    b. Prior agreements

      (1) Cancelled

      (2) Suspended

      (3) Incorporated by reference

II. Grant of Patent Rights

A. Exclusive (or nonexclusive)

B. General limitations

1. Make, use, sell, or lease

2. Have made

3. Less than all claims

C. Territorial limitations

  1. Geographical

  2. Plant location

D. Field-of-use limitations

  1. Style or size of product

  2. Sale solely in specified combination

  3. Sale for limited uses

  4. Sale limited to prescribed customers

  5. Sale for use in limited areas

  6. Sale through specified trade channels

III. Royalties

A. Fixed royalty

  1. Lump sum

  2. Fixed sum payable in installments

  3. Fixed periodic payments

  4. Interest on overdue payments

  5. Acceleration on default

B. Running royalty

  1. Rate

    a. Direct proportion (proportion)

    b. Descending

    c. Ascending

  2. Base

    a. Number of units

      (1) Manufactured, sold, or processed

      (2) Definition of "sold"

      (3) One payment per unit

    b. Supplies or raw materials used

      (1) Volume basis

      (2) Cost basis

    c. Use compensation received by licensee

    d. Net sales of licensee

      (1) Definition of "sold"

      (2) Definition of "net sales"

3. Related matters

    a. Interest on overdue payments

    b. Effect of termination on obligation to pay accrued royalties

4. Minimum payments

    a. Supplementary initial payment

      (1) Independent of future royalties

      (2) Credited against future royalties

    b. Minimum royalties

      (1) Payment mandatory

      (2) Payment optional

        (a) To retain exclusiveness

        (b) To maintain license

5. Accounting matters

    a. Time and content of royalty reports

    b. Time of royalty payments

c. Maintenance of records

d. Examination of records

    (1) Licensor or independent accountant

    (2) Time limitation

    (3) Information confidential

    (4) After termination

IV. Other Principal Rights and Obligations

A. Release for past infringement

  1. Licensee; licensee's customers

  2. Absolute or conditioned

    a. On continuance of agreement

    b. On payment of prescribed sum

  3. Specific or general release

B. Warranties by licensor

  1. Ownership of licensed patent

  2. Right to license

C. Most favored licensee

  1. Scope of clause

    a. All terms generally

    b. Royalty terms only

  2. Application of more favorable terms

    a. Automatically

    b. At licensee's option

  3. Original licensee entitled to

    a. Notification of later license

    b. Copy of later license

D. Sublicensing

    1. Prohibited

    2. Permitted

E. Acknowledgment of validity

    1. Agreement not to assist others in contesting validity

F. Admission of infringement

    1. General admission

    2. Specific to identified devices

G. Enforcement of licensed patent

    1. Right or obligation of

        a. Licensor

        b. Licensee

        c. Parties jointly

    2. Allocation of expenses and recoveries

    3. Inaction or default by one party

        a. Enforcement by other party

        b. Termination of agreement by other party

        c. Cancellation of exclusiveness by licensor

        d. Cessation of royalty payments by licensee

H. Invalidity of licensed patent

    1. Claim is invalidated

        a. Right to terminate agreement

        b. Effect on royalty payments

    2. Claims construed: Effect on royalty payments

I. Know-how and technical assistance

    1. Furnishing of information

        a. Present; future

b. Written material only

c. Only information licensor has right to divulge

d. Maintenance of secrecy

   (1) Restrictions on use

   (2) Agreements with employees

   (3) Indemnification for breach

e. Termination of license

   (1) Return of tangible material

   (2) Continuance of secrecy

2. Visitation rights of licensee and training of licensee's personnel

   a. Time limitations

   b. Expenses of training

3. Furnishing advisory services

   a. Time limitations

   b. Compensation for licensor

J. Patent marking

   1. As specified by statute

   2. As specified in agreement

K. Defense of infringement suits

   1. By licensor

      a. Defend only; indemnify also

      b. Licensee; licensee's customers

      c. Liability dependent on

         (1) Prompt notification

         (2) Cooperation

      d. Liability limited to

         (1) Arbitrary amount

(2) Compensation received from licensee

2. By licensee

  a. Expenses offset against royalties payable licensor

  b. Liability of licensor limited to cooperation

3. By parties jointly

  a. Allocation of expenses

  b. Responsibility for conduct of defense

L. Improvements

1. By licensor; inclusion in license

  a. Automatically

  b. Adoption by licensee

2. By licensee

  a. Inclusion in primary license for royalty purposes

  b. License to licensor

  c. Assignment to licensor

3. By parties jointly

  a. Joint ownership maintained

  b. Allocation of patent prosecution expenses

  c. Inclusion in primary license for royalty purposes

4. Related matters

  a. Definition of "improvement"

  b. Invention agreements with key employees

M. Prosecution of licensed application

1. Responsibility for prosecution

  a. Direction of prosecution

  b. Expenses of prosecution

2. Effect of nonallowance of claims on royalty payments

V. Duration, Termination, and Subsidiary Formal Provisions

A. Duration

    1. Effective date

    2. Term

        a. Life of patent

        b. Specified period

        c. Initial period subject to renewal

    3. Option to cancel

        a. At any time on notice

        b. Within an initial period

        c. After a stated period

B. Termination for cause

    1. By licensor

        a. Any default of licensee

        b. Bankruptcy, etc., of licensee

        c. Nonpayment of royalties

        d. Nonpayment of minimum royalties

        e. Failure to render royalty and production reports

        f. Failure to enforce patent

    2. By licensee

        a. Any default of licensor

        b. Failure to enforce patent

        c. Claims held invalid

    3. Manner of effecting

        a. Notice of default

        b. Period to remedy

        c. Notice of termination

4. Preservation of other rights and remedies at law and in equity

C. Post-transaction

  1. Right of licensee

    a. Sale of products on hand

    b. Limitation in time or units

  2. Obligations of licensee

    a. Payment of accrued royalties

    b. Payment of royalties on authorized post-termination sales

    c. Return of know-how in tangible form

    d. Continued maintenance of know-how secret

  3. Rights of licensor

    a. Purchase of licensee's products on hand

    b. Examination of licensee's books and records

D. Severability of provisions

E. Arbitration

  1. Arbitrable disputes

    a. All disputes

    b. Specific disputes only

  2. Optional or exclusive remedy

  3. Arbitrators

    a. Number

    b. Manner of selection

  4. Place of hearing

  5. Majority or unanimous award

  6. Governing rules

F. Limitation on effect of waiver

G. Agency and similar relationships

    1. Negation of such relationships

    2. Statement that licensee is independent contractor

    3. Agreement by licensee not to act for licensor

H. Entire agreement and modifications

    1. Merger of prior discussions

    2. Negation of implied warranties

    3. Written modifications only

I. Assignment

    1. Authorized

        a. One or both parties

        b. Limitations

        c. Release of assignor from liability

        d. Assumption of obligations by assignee

    2. Prohibited

J. Governing law

K. Notices

    1. Written

    2. Manner of service

    3. When effective

L. Execution of agreement

    1. Recital of execution

    2. Date of execution

    3. Signatures of parties

Royalty Rates by Industry

Industry	Average (%)	Median (%)
Automotive	4.7	4.0
Chemicals	4.7	3.6
Computer Hardware	5.2	4.0
Computer Software	10.5	6.8
Consumer Goods	5.5	5.0
Electronics	4.3	4.0
Food	2.9	2.8
Internet	11.7	7.5
Healthcare Products	5.8	4.8
Machines/Tools	5.2	4.5
Pharmaceuticals & Biotech	7.0	5.1
Semiconductors	4.6	3.2
Telecom	5.3	4.7

Confidentiality and Nondisclosure Agreement*

THIS AGREEMENT is made the ____ day of _____, 20___, by and between _____, a _____[company type, e.g., a corporation] organized and existing under the laws of the State of _____, having a principal place of business at _____ ("Disclosing Party"), and _____, [company type, if applicable] [organized and existing under the laws of the State of _____, if applicable], having a principal place of business at [if business, or] with offices at _____ ("Recipient").

WHEREAS, Disclosing Party is the proprietor of information concerning _____ (the "Information"); and

WHEREAS, Recipient is interested to learn the Information so as to be able to determine their interest in the use of the Information [or, in connection with _____ project].

NOW, THEREFORE, in consideration of mutual premises and covenants, it is mutually agreed as follows.

1. Disclosing Party agrees to divulge to Recipient sufficient details of the Information to enable Recipient to understand the substance thereof. It is mutually understood that, unless otherwise specifically indicated in

---

* Note: This document is presented for illustrative purposes only. The reader is strongly encouraged to consult with a professional before entering into any license or other contract.

writing, any information so communicated by Disclosing Party to Recipient is confidential and constitutes valuable trade secrets of Disclosing Party.

2.   In order to induce Disclosing Party to divulge the Information, Recipient covenants and warrants (i) to use the Information only for the purposes hereinabove stated, (ii) not to use any of the Information for the Recipient's own benefit, and (iii) not to disclose any of it to third parties without the prior written permission of Disclosing Party.

3.   Excluded from the above restriction is any part of Disclosing Party's disclosure that:

> a. can be demonstrated to have been in the public domain prior to the date hereof;
>
> b. can be demonstrated to have been in Recipient's possession prior to the date hereof;
>
> c. becomes part of the public domain by publication or otherwise, not due to any unauthorized act or omission on Recipient's part; or
>
> d. is supplied to Recipient by any third party as a matter of right insofar as the Information had been obtained by such third party lawfully.

4.   The rights and obligations herein are personal to Disclosing Party and Recipient and cannot be assigned without the prior written permission of the other party. This Agreement contains the entire understanding of the parties relating to the matters referred to herein, and can be amended only by a written instrument duly executed on behalf of Disclosing Party and Recipient.

IN WITNESS WHEREOF, the parties hereto have caused this Agreement to be duly executed as of the date hereinabove set forth.

_____ [Disclosing Party]

By: _____

Name, Title

_____ [Recipient]

By: _____

Name [Title, if applicable]

Trademark License Agreement*

LICENSE AGREEMENT

THIS AGREEMENT (hereinafter referred to as the "Agreement") entered into this _____ day of _____, 20___, by and between _____, a corporation organized and existing under the laws of _____ and having a place of business at _____ (hereinafter referred to as "Licensor"), and _____, having a place of business at _____ (hereinafter referred to as "Licensee");

    WHEREAS, Licensor is the owner of the entire right, title, and interest in and to the trademark(s) _____ (hereinafter referred to as "Trademark(s)"); and

    WHEREAS, Licensee is desirous of obtaining a license from Licensor to use the Trademark(s) on _____ and/or packaging therefore;

    NOW, THEREFORE, the parties agree as follows:

---

* Note: This document is presented for illustrative purposes only. The reader is strongly encouraged to consult with a professional before entering into any license or other contract.

1. GRANT

    1.1   Licensor grants to Licensee, subject to the terms and conditions set forth in this agreement, nonexclusive, nontransferable, nonassignable rights for the period effective on _____ and ending _____ to use the Trademark(s) on _____ and packaging therefor to be sold by Licensee in the United States only.

    1.2   Licensee shall have no right to sublicense any rights granted herein without the prior written consent of Licensor.

2. LICENSEE FEES

    2.1   Licensee shall pay to Licensor a license fee for articles covered by this Agreement equal to _____ percent (_____%) of Licensee's net selling price of each article.

    2.2   For the purpose of computing license fees under this Agreement, net selling price shall be the invoice price charged by Licensee to its customers for the licensed articles sold under this Agreement, less any credit for returns.

    2.3   No costs incurred by Licensee in manufacturing, selling, advertising, or distribution of the licensed articles, or overhead or indirect expenses or losses on uncollectible accounts shall be allowed as deductions.

    2.4   Sales shall be considered to have been made when the product is shipped to the customer.

    2.5   Licensee shall make an annual payment of _____ ($_____) which shall be due upon execution and delivery of this Agreement, and again upon subsequent anniversary dates of this Agreement or any renewals or extensions thereof. The annual payment shall be applied against subsequent license fee payments as earned, as a result of sales by Licensee of the licensed articles sold under this Agreement solely during the calendar year immediately subsequent to such annual payment.

3. ACCOUNTING

3.1 Licensee, within thirty (30) days after the end of each calendar quarter, any part of which falls within the term of this Agreement, shall furnish Licensor with a written statement specifying the total number of articles sold and the net selling price per article for licensed articles sold under this Agreement during the immediately preceding quarter.

3.2 Each such statement specified in Para. 3.1 shall be accompanied by the payment of any additional license fee not covered by the annual payment set forth in Para. 2.5, and such statement shall be made even if no additional license fee is due.

3.3 Licensee agrees to keep complete books and records showing sales of articles covered by this Agreement, which books and records shall be open to inspection during normal working hours by a certified public accountant acceptable to Licensor and Licensee for the purpose of verifying the license fee statements set forth in Para. 3.1. All such books and records shall be kept available for at least two (2) years after termination of the calendar year to which they relate.

3.4 In order to facilitate inspection of the books and records for verifying license fee statements, Licensee agrees to designate a symbol or number which will be used exclusively in connection with the licensed articles.

4. QUALITY CONTROL

4.1 Before Licensee sells any article under this Agreement, Licensee shall submit two samples of each type of licensed article sold under this Agreement for approval as to the quality thereof, the proper use of the Trademark(s), and compliance with other terms and conditions of this Agreement. Approval shall be inferred if Licensor makes no written objection within twenty (20) days of receipt of said samples.

4.2 Licensee recognizes that the manner in which Licensee uses the licensed Trademark(s) could have a significant effect on Licensor's quality image. Therefore, Licensee promises to maintain the same quality in the articles produced and sold as in the samples submitted by Licensee and approved by Licensor, and Licensee agrees to supply, from time to time and upon written request from Licensor, representative samples of the licensed articles to Licensor for quality verification.

4.3 Original artwork, including promotional advertising, shall be submitted to Licensor for approval. If, during the term of this Agreement, there is any change in the artwork or in the articles, any such change shall be submitted to Licensor and must be approved by Licensor in writing before being put into effect by Licensee.

5. SOURCE IDENTIFICATION

5.1 Licensee shall place its own name or identifying mark on the articles and/or packaging in an inconspicuous manner so that the origin of the articles can be determined.

6. TRADEMARK OWNERSHIP

6.1 Licensee recognizes that Licensor is the owner of and has the right to use the Trademark(s) covered by this Agreement, and further agrees that Licensee's use of the Trademark(s) under the terms and conditions of this Agreement shall inure to the benefit of Licensor.

6.2 Licensee agrees to cooperate with the Licensor to the extent required and as requested by Licensor to enable Licensor to secure any desired registration of the Trademark(s) for the licensed articles.

6.3 Licensee shall not use any language or display the Trademark(s) in such a way as to create the impression that the Trademark(s) are the property of Licensee.

6.4 Licensee expressly waives any and all claims to any rights to or in the Trademark(s), whether of trademark, trade name, copyright, or otherwise, beyond the limited permission to the use herein granted.

6.5 Licensee shall have no right to use the Trademark(s) on any article or articles other than those specifically listed in this Agreement or on packaging, advertising, and promotional materials used in connection with the sale of said articles.

7. RIGHTS TO INDEMNIFICATION

7.1 Licensee acknowledges that it will have no claim against Licensor for indemnification of any damages or other losses that it may incur as a result of any allegations or claims of patent, trademark, copyright, or other infringements brought against Licensee by any third parties arising out of the use of the Trademark(s) by Licensee.

7.2 Licensee agrees to defend, indemnify, and save Licensor, its directors, officers, agents, or employees harmless from any and all costs, including but not limited to attorneys' fees incurred in connection with any claim of damage or injury to property or persons brought or assessed against Licensor, its directors, officers, agents, or employees and arising out of the conduct of Licensee's business or use of the licensed articles by third parties.

7.3 Licensee shall obtain, display to Licensor, and maintain product liability insurance providing protection for Licensor, its directors, officers, agents, or employees, against any costs, expenses, claims, demands, or causes of action and resulting settlements, awards, or judgments arising out of any alleged defects in the licensed articles or any use thereof. Such product liability insurance shall be in the amount of _____ ($_____) for each and every such claim, demand, or cause of action and resulting settlements, awards, or judgments.

8. TERMINATION

8.1 In the event that Licensee breaches any of the provisions of this Agreement, Licensor shall have the right to immediately terminate this Agreement upon written notice. In that event, Licensee shall have sixty (60) days from the date of termination to dispose of its entire inventory of products covered by this Agreement. Such termination shall not relieve Licensee from the obligation of paying the required license fee for all goods sold under the licensed Trademark(s).

8.2 The sixty- (60-) day disposal period referred to above shall not take effect in the event that this Agreement is terminated for failure of Licensee to maintain the required quality of the licensed articles, in which case Licensee agrees to destroy all such licensed articles in its possession at the time of such termination, or obliterate the Trademark(s) therefrom, and make no further sales thereof.

8.3 Upon termination or expiration of this or any subsequent related Agreements, Licensee agrees that it will not use the Trademark(s) licensed hereunder or any other trademarks confusingly similar thereto on any of its products without the express written permission of Licensor. Licensee agrees that its failure to adhere to this provision shall inflict irreparable injury to Licensor's reputation and goodwill, and agrees that preliminary and permanent injunctive and other equitable relief would be appropriate in the event of such failure to adhere to this provision.

8.4 This Agreement shall automatically terminate in the event that Licensee shall make any assignment for the benefit of creditors, or shall file any petition under Chapter 10, 11, or 12 of Title 11, United States Code (or any similar law which might be applicable to Licensee or its business), or file a voluntary petition in bankruptcy, or be adjudicated a bankrupt or insolvent, or if any receiver is appointed for its business or property, or if any trustee in bankruptcy or insolvency shall be appointed for it.

9. NOTICES

9.1 Notices provided for herein shall be considered effectively given when sent by certified mail in the case of Licensor to:

in the case of Licensee to:

10. RELATIONSHIP OF THE PARTIES

10.1 It is agreed and understood that Licensee is an independent con-
tractor and not an agent or employee of Licensor and has no
right to hold itself out as an agent or employee of Licensor.

10.2 Licensee has no right to assume or create any obligation or liability of any nature, express or implied, in the name of Licensor.

10.3 Licensor has no proprietary interest in Licensee and has no interest
in the business of Licensee, except to the extent set forth in this
Agreement.

11. CONSTRUCTION OF AGREEMENT

11.1 This Agreement shall be construed in accordance with the laws
of the State of _____.

12. RENEWAL

12.1 This Agreement may be renewed or extended only upon the
prior written consent of both the parties.

IN WITNESS WHEREOF, we have caused our signatures and corporate seals to be affixed hereto by the below indicated duly authorized officers.

For and on behalf of
[Licensor]

_____ Date: _____

By: _____

Title: _____

For and on behalf of
[Licensee]

_____ Date: _____

By: _____

Title: _____

Patent License Agreement (Paid-Up)*

THIS AGREEMENT (hereinafter referred to as the "Agreement") is made by and between Licensor Company (hereinafter referred to as "Licensor"), a _____ [form of organization] with principal offices at _____, and _____, a _____ with principal offices at _____ (hereinafter referred to as "Licensee").

WITNESSETH:

WHEREAS, Licensor is the owner of all right, title, and interest in United States Patent Nos. _____ (which patents are hereinafter collectively referred to as the "Licensed Patents");

WHEREAS, Licensee is in the business of making and selling _____, and desires to obtain a nonexclusive license to make, use, and sell products and to practice the inventions covered by the Licensed Patents;

WHEREAS, Licensor and Licensee desire to enter into a license agreement covering the Licensed Patents; and

WHEREAS, Licensor has the right to grant a nonexclusive license to Licensee under the Licensed Patents and is willing to do so on the terms and conditions recited in this Agreement.

---

* Note: This document is presented for illustrative purposes only. The reader is strongly encouraged to consult with a professional before entering into any license or other contract.

NOW, THEREFORE, in consideration of the preceding and the mutual covenants recited below, and for other good and valuable consideration, receipt and sufficiency of which is hereby acknowledged, the parties agree as follows:

1. DEFINITIONS

1.1 Licensed Patents. "Licensed Patents" as used in this Agreement shall mean the _____, collectively, and any patent issued in the future from any reissue, reexamination, divisional, continuation, and/or continuation-in-part of the Licensed Patents, including any foreign counterpart thereof.

1.2 Territory. "Territory" as used in this Agreement shall mean the United States and its territories and possessions. [If foreign patents are licensed, include respective countries.]

1.3 Effective Date. "Effective Date" shall mean _____, 20___.

1.4 Term. "Term" as used in this Agreement shall mean the period beginning on the Effective Date and ending with the expiration of the last to expire of the Licensed Patents or the termination of this Agreement, whichever occurs first. This Agreement shall, if not terminated sooner, terminate at the end of the Term.

1.5 Licensed Product. "Licensed Product" as used in this Agreement shall mean certain _____ made, used, imported, sold, or offered for sale by Licensee, including, but not limited to: _____.

1.6 Past Products. "Past Products" as used in this Agreement shall mean the Licensed Products made or sold by Licensee before the Effective Date of this Agreement.

2. LICENSE

2.1 License Grant. Subject to the terms and conditions of this Agreement and the due performance by Licensee of Licensee's obligations under this Agreement and in reliance on Licensee's representations and warranties set forth in this Agreement, Licensor hereby grants to Licensee a personal, nonexclusive, non-transferable limited license under the Licensed Patents for the Term in the Territory to make, use, import, offer to sell, and sell Licensed Products and Past Products, with no right to sublicense. This license shall not extend to any third party, subsidiary, division, or any entity acquired after the Effective Date.

2.2 Basis. The foregoing license is granted solely under the Licensed Patents. No license under any other patents or intellectual property of Licensor is granted, either expressly or by implication.

2.3 Marking. During the Term of this Agreement, Licensee shall affix to Licensed Products a statement in substantially the form: "U.S. Patent Nos. _____." The Licensee shall provide Licensor with the samples of its Licensed Products evidencing proper marking as required hereunder. From time to time, and within a reasonable time after written notice from Licensor, Licensor shall have the right to inspect Licensee's Licensed Products to determine if Licensee is marking in accordance with this paragraph.

3. PAYMENTS

3.1 Paid-up License. For the rights granted in this Agreement Licensee shall unconditionally pay Licensor a one-time license fee of _____and 00/100 Dollars ($_____.00), which shall be due immediately upon the Effective Date and payable within three (3) days of the Effective Date.

3.2 Confidentiality. Licensor and Licensee acknowledge that the amount of Licensee's payments actually made to Licensor under this Agreement is confidential and proprietary information relating to this Agreement and the business of Licensor and Licensee. Accordingly, the parties agree that each of them shall keep that information confidential and shall not disclose it, or permit it to be disclosed, to any third party (other than to agents or representatives who need to know such information). Licensor shall have the right, however, to disclose that Licensor and Licensee have entered into this Agreement, the royalty rate(s) set forth in this Agreement, that Licensee is paying for Past Products, and that Licensee has consented to the validity, enforceability, and infringement of the Licensed Patents.

4. INDEMNIFICATION

4.1 Licensee Indemnification. Licensee shall at all times during the term of this Agreement and thereafter indemnify, defend, and hold Licensor, its directors, officers, employees, and affiliates harmless against all claims, proceedings, demands, and liabilities of any kind whatsoever, including legal expenses and reasonable attorneys' fees, arising out of the death of or injury to any person or out of any damage to property, or resulting from the production, manufacture, sale, use, lease, or advertisement of Licensed Products or Past Products or arising from any obligation of Licensee under this Agreement.

4.2 Licensor Indemnification. Licensor shall at all times during the term of this Agreement and thereafter indemnify, defend, and hold Licensee, its directors, officers, employees, and affiliates harmless against all claims, proceedings, demands, and liabilities of any kind whatsoever, including legal expenses and reasonable attorneys' fees, arising out of any breach of any representation, warranty, or covenant expressly made by Licensor in this Agreement.

5. TERMINATION

5.1 Termination by Licensor. In addition to all other remedies Licensor may have, Licensor may terminate this Agreement and the licenses granted in this Agreement in the event that:

(a) Licensee defaults in its payment to Licensor and such default continues unremedied for a period of thirty (30) days after the Effective Date of this Agreement;

(b) Licensee fails to perform any material obligation, warranty, duty, or responsibility or is in default with respect to any term or condition undertaken by Licensee hereunder, and such failure or default continues unremedied for a period of thirty (30) days after written notice thereof to Licensee by Licensor;

(c) Licensee is liquidated or dissolved;

(d) Any assignment is made of Licensee's business for the benefit of creditors;

(e) Licensee liquidates a substantial portion of its business or engages in a distress sale of substantially all of its assets;

(f) A receiver, or similar officer, is appointed to take charge of a substantial part of Licensee's assets;

(g) Licensee is unable to pay its debts as they mature; or

(h) Any petition in bankruptcy is filed by or against Licensee that remains undischarged for sixty (60) days.

5.2 Termination by Licensee. If all the Licensed Patents are determined to be invalid or unenforceable by any court or tribunal of competent jurisdiction, and the determination becomes final in that it is not further reviewable through appeal or exhaustion of all permissible petitions or applications for rehearing or review, Licensee may terminate this Agreement at will and shall have no further obligations hereunder.

5.3 Effect of Termination. After the termination of this Agreement, Licensee shall have no rights under the Licensed Patents.

5.4 No Discharge on Termination. No termination of this Agreement for any reason shall relieve or discharge either Licensor or Licensee from any duty, obligation, or liability that was accrued as of the date of the termination (including, without limitation, the obligation to indemnify or to pay any amounts owing as of the date of termination).

6. REPRESENTATIONS AND WARRANTIES OF LICENSOR

6.1 Right to Grant License. Licensor represents and warrants that Licensor has the right and authority to grant the licenses granted to Licensee in this Agreement and that this Agreement and the licenses granted in this Agreement do not and will not conflict with the terms of any agreement to which Licensor is a party.

6.2 Disclaimers. Except as otherwise expressly set forth in this Agreement, Licensor, its directors, officers, employees, and agents make no representations and extend no warranties of any kind, either express or implied. In particular, and without limitation, nothing in this Agreement shall be construed as:

(a) a warranty or representation by Licensor as to the validity or scope of the Licensed Patents;

(b) a warranty or representation by Licensor that anything made, used, sold, or otherwise disposed of under any license granted in this Agreement is or will be free from infringement of patents of third parties;

(c) an obligation on the part of Licensor to bring or prosecute actions against third parties for infringement of the Licensed Patents or other proprietary rights;

(d) an obligation on the part of Licensor to furnish any manufacturing or technical information;

(e) the granting by implication, estoppel, or otherwise of any licenses or rights under patents other than the Licensed Patents; or

(f) the assumption by Licensor of any responsibilities whatever with respect to use, sale, or other disposition by Licensee or its vendees or transferees of Licensed Products.

6.3 Limitation of Liability. In no event shall Licensor, its directors, officers, employees, or affiliates be liable for incidental or consequential damages of any kind, including economic damage or injury to property and lost profits, regardless of whether Licensor shall be advised, shall have other reason to know, or in fact shall know of the possibility.

7. REPRESENTATIONS AND WARRANTIES OF LICENSEE

Licensee represents and warrants that Licensee has the right and authority to enter into this Agreement and that this Agreement and the exercise of the licenses granted hereunder do not and will not conflict with the terms of any agreement to which Licensee is a party. Except as otherwise expressly set forth in this Agreement, Licensee, its directors, officers, employees, and agents make no representations and extend no warranties of any kind, either express or implied. In particular, and without limitation, nothing in this Agreement shall be construed as an obligation on the part of Licensee to furnish any manufacturing or technical information.

8. RELATIONSHIP OF THE PARTIES

Nothing in this Agreement will be construed to constitute the parties as partners or joint venturers or constitute either party as agent of the other, nor will any similar relationship be deemed to exist between them. Neither party shall hold itself out contrary to the terms of this paragraph and neither party shall become liable by reason of any representation, act, or omission of the other contrary to the provisions of this paragraph. This Agreement is not for the benefit of any third party and shall not be deemed to give any right or remedy to any such party, whether referred to in this Agreement or not.

9. ASSIGNMENT

9.1 No Assignment. This Agreement, the rights granted to Licensee, and the duties and obligations of Licensee are all personal to Licensee and Licensee agrees not to sell, assign, transfer, mortgage, pledge, or hypothecate any such rights in whole or in part, or delegate any of its duties or obligations under this Agreement; nor shall any of Licensee's rights or duties be assigned, transferred, or delegated by Licensee to any third party by operation of law. Any purported transfer, assignment, or delegation in violation of the foregoing sentence shall be void and without effect, and this Agreement shall thereupon become terminable without further notice by Licensor. In the context of this provision, "assignment" shall include the transfer of substantially all of the assets of Licensee, or of a majority interest in the voting stock of Licensee, or the merger, consolidation, or reorganization of Licensee with one or more third parties.

9.2 Binding on Successors. This Agreement will inure to the benefit of and be binding upon Licensor, its successors, and assigns.

10. DISPUTE RESOLUTION

10.1 Arbitration of Royalty Disputes.

(a) Any dispute between Licensor and Licensee concerning the amount of royalties payable to Licensor under this Agreement shall be submitted for binding arbitration in accordance with the provisions of this Section 10 and the then-applicable rules of the American Arbitration Association (the "Association"). Judgment upon the arbitration award may be entered in any court of competent jurisdiction.

(b) The power of the arbitrators shall be limited to resolving the specific issues stated by determining the royalties Licensee owes or should receive credit for, if any, under this Agreement. The power of the arbitrators shall not extend to any other matters. All other disputes shall be subject to litigation in a court of competent jurisdiction.

(c) The arbitration panel or tribunal shall consist solely of neutral arbitrators.

(d) The parties agree that arbitration proceedings under this Agreement shall not be stayed on the ground of pending litigation to which either or both of them is a party.

10.2 Remedies. Except as expressly provided herein, all specific remedies provided for in this Agreement are cumulative and are not exclusive of one another or of any other remedies available in law or equity.

11. LIMITATIONS OF RIGHTS AND AUTHORITY

11.1 Limitation of Rights. No right or title whatsoever in the Licensed Patents is granted by Licensor to Licensee, or shall be taken or assumed by Licensee, except as is specifically set forth in this Agreement.

11.2 Limitation of Authority. Neither party shall, in any respect whatsoever, be taken to be the agent or representative of the other party, and neither party shall have any authority to assume any obligation for the other party, or to commit the other party in any way.

12. MISCELLANEOUS

12.1 Computation of Time. The time in which any act provided in this Agreement is to be done shall be computed by excluding the first day and including the last day, unless the last day is a Saturday, Sunday, or legal holiday, and then it shall also be excluded.

12.2 Notices. All notices given in connection with this Agreement shall be in writing and shall be deemed given upon actual receipt by the addressee. Notices shall be personally delivered or sent by telex or facsimile (with prompt confirmation by registered or certified air mail, postage prepaid) or by registered or certified air mail, postage prepaid, addressed to the party to be notified at the following address, or at such other address as the party may designate by notice:

Licensor:

_____

_____

_____

Attention: _____

Phone: _____

Facsimile: _____

Licensee:

_____

_____

_____

Attention: _____

Phone: _____

Facsimile: _____

12.3 Survival. The provisions of this Agreement relating to payment obligations, confidentiality, indemnification, remedies, and arbitration shall survive the expiration or termination of this Agreement.

12.4 Severability. If any provision of this Agreement is declared by a court of competent jurisdiction to be invalid, illegal, unenforceable, or void then both parties shall be relieved of all obligations arising under such provision, but only to the extent that such provision is invalid, illegal, unenforceable, or void. If the remainder of this Agreement is capable of substantial performance, then each provision not so affected shall be enforced to the extent permitted by law.

12.5 Waiver and Modification. No modification of any of the terms of this Agreement will be valid unless in writing and signed by both parties. No waiver by either party of a breach of this Agreement will be deemed a waiver by such party of any subsequent breach.

12.6 Headings. The headings in this Agreement are for reference only and shall not in any way control the meaning or interpretation of this Agreement.

12.7 Interpretation. No provision of this Agreement is to be interpreted for or against any party because that party or its attorney drafted the provision.

12.8 Governing Law. This Agreement shall be construed, governed, interpreted, and applied in accordance with the laws of the State of _____.

12.9 No Other Agreement. The parties each represent that in entering into this Agreement, they rely on no promise, inducement, or other agreement not expressly contained in this Agreement; that they have read this Agreement and discussed it thoroughly with their respective legal counsel; that they understand all of the provisions of this Agreement and intend to be bound by them; and that they enter into this Agreement voluntarily.

12.10 Entire Agreement. This Agreement constitutes the complete and exclusive statement of the terms and conditions between the parties, which supersedes and merges all prior proposals, understandings, and all other agreements, oral and written, between the parties relating to the subject of this Agreement.

12.11 Counterparts. This Agreement may be executed in counterparts, which taken together shall constitute one document.

IN WITNESS WHEREOF, the parties have executed this Agreement by their duly authorized representatives.

For and on behalf of
[Licensor]

_____   Date: _____, 20____

By: _____

Title: _____

For and on behalf of
[Licensee]

_____   Date: _____, 20____

By:_____

Title: _____

Patent License Agreement (Running Royalty)*

THIS AGREEMENT (hereinafter referred to as the "Agreement") is made by and between Licensor Company (hereinafter referred to as "Licensor "), a _____ [form of organization] with principal offices at _____, and _____, a _____ with principal offices at _____ (hereinafter referred to as "Licensee").

W I T N E S S E T H:

WHEREAS, Licensor is the owner of all right, title, and interest in United States Patent Nos. _____ (which patents are hereinafter collectively referred to as the "Licensed Patents");

WHEREAS, Licensee is in the business of making and selling _____, and desires to obtain a nonexclusive license to make, use, and sell products and to practice the inventions covered by the Licensed Patents;

WHEREAS, Licensor and Licensee desire to enter into a license agreement covering the Licensed Patents; and

WHEREAS, Licensor has the right to grant a nonexclusive license to Licensee under the Licensed Patents and is willing to do so on the terms and conditions recited in this Agreement.

---

* Note: This document is presented for illustrative purposes only. The reader is strongly encouraged to consult with a professional before entering into any license or other contract.

NOW, THEREFORE, in consideration of the preceding and the mutual covenants recited below, and for other good and valuable consideration, receipt and sufficiency of which is hereby acknowledged, the parties agree as follows:

1. DEFINITIONS

   1.1 **Licensed Patents.** "Licensed Patents" as used in this Agreement shall mean the _____, collectively, and any patent issued in the future from any reissue, reexamination, divisional, continuation, and/or continuation-in-part of the Licensed Patents, including any foreign counterpart thereof.

   1.2 **Territory.** "Territory" as used in this Agreement shall mean the United States and its territories and possessions. [If foreign patents are licensed, include respective countries.]

   1.3 **Effective Date.** "Effective Date" shall mean _____, __.

   1.4 **Term.** "Term" as used in this Agreement shall mean the period beginning on the Effective Date and ending with the expiration of the last to expire of the Licensed Patents or the termination of this Agreement, whichever occurs first. This Agreement shall, if not terminated sooner, terminate at the end of the Term.

   1.5 **Licensed Product.** "Licensed Product" as used in this Agreement shall mean certain _____ made, used, imported, sold, or offered for sale by Licensee, including, but not limited to: _____.

   1.6 **Past Products.** "Past Products" as used in this Agreement shall mean the Licensed Products made or sold by Licensee before the Effective Date of this Agreement.

2. LICENSE

2.1 License Grant. Subject to the terms and conditions of this Agreement and the due performance by Licensee of Licensee's obligations under this Agreement and in reliance on Licensee's representations and warranties set forth in this Agreement, Licensor hereby grants to Licensee a personal, nonexclusive, non-transferable limited license under the Licensed Patents for the Term in the Territory to make, use, import, offer to sell, and sell Licensed Products and Past Products, with no right to sublicense. This license shall not extend to any third party, subsidiary, division, or any entity acquired after the Effective Date.

2.2 Basis. The foregoing license is granted solely under the Licensed Patents. No license under any other patents or intellectual property of Licensor is granted, either expressly or by implication.

2.3 Marking. During the Term of this Agreement, Licensee shall affix to Licensed Products a statement in substantially the form: "U.S. Patent Nos. _____." The Licensee shall provide Licensor with the samples of its Licensed Products evidencing proper marking as required hereunder. From time to time, and within a reasonable time after written notice from Licensor, Licensor shall have the right to inspect Licensee's Licensed Products to determine if Licensee is marking in accordance with this paragraph.

3. PAYMENTS

3.1 Running Royalty.

3.1.1 Royalty Payment. For the rights granted in this Agreement, and subject to Paragraphs 3.2 and 3.3 herein below, Licensee shall pay Licensor a royalty of ___ percent (__%) of Licensee's selling price for each Licensed

Product manufactured, used, or sold by Licensee in the Territory or imported by Licensee into the Territory.

3.1.2 Termination of Royalty on Invalidity or Unenforceability. The royalty payments shall terminate if all of the Licensed Patents are held invalid or unenforceable. A Licensed Patent shall be deemed invalid or unenforceable under this Agreement if a court or tribunal of competent jurisdiction makes such a determination, and the determination becomes final in that it is not further reviewable through appeal or exhaustion of all permissible petitions or applications for rehearing or review.

3.2 Accrual. A running royalty as to a unit of Licensed Product shall accrue on the day the unit is shipped or invoiced to a Licensee customer, whichever occurs first.

3.3 Payment. All royalty payments to Licensor shall be made quarterly by Licensee, with the first quarter being defined as January 1 through March 31, the second quarter as April 1 through June 30, the third quarter as July 1 through September 30, and the fourth quarter as October 1 through December 31. Payment of royalties shall be made to Licensor not later than the thirtieth (30th) day (the "Due Date") after the end of the period to which the payment relates. Each royalty payment as defined herein above shall be subject to and be no less than a minimum royalty of _____ Dollars ($_____) per quarter.

3.4 Accounting Statements. Licensee shall provide Licensor with a statement of royalties due Licensor under this Agreement quarterly (as that term is defined in Paragraph 3.3) on or before the Due Date, setting forth the amount due to Licensor for the period and, in reasonable detail, the factual basis for calculating the amount.

3.5 **Interest.** Subject to the limits imposed by any applicable usury law, interest shall accrue on payments made more than ten (10) days after they are due at the rate of _____ percent (__%) per annum, compounded daily, from the due date until paid.

3.6 **Books and Records and Audit.** Licensee shall keep full, complete, and accurate books of account and records covering all transactions relating to this Agreement. Licensee shall preserve such books and records for a period of three (3) years after the Due Date to which the material relates. Acceptance by Licensor of an accounting statement or payment hereunder will not preclude Licensor from challenging or questioning the accuracy thereof. During the Term and for a period of one (1) year thereafter, Licensor may, upon reasonable notice in writing to Licensee, cause an independent audit to be made of the books and records of Licensee in order to verify the statements rendered under this Agreement, and prompt adjustment shall be made by the proper party to compensate for any errors disclosed by the audit. The audit shall be conducted only by an independent accountant during regular business hours and in a reasonable manner so as not to interfere with normal business activities. Audits shall be made hereunder no more frequently than annually. Before any audit may be conducted, the auditor must represent that the auditor's fee will in no manner be determined by the results of the audit and must agree to maintain the confidentiality of all confidential material to which the auditor is given access. Licensor will bear all expenses and fees of the audit, but if the audit reveals an underpayment for any quarter of more than five percent (5%), Licensee shall pay all such expenses and fees. Licensee shall provide samples of any new _____, and/or a complete written description thereof, sufficient to enable Licensor to determine whether such product is covered by any of the claims of any of the Licensed Patents.

3.7 Confidentiality. Licensor and Licensee acknowledge that the amount of Licensee's payments actually made to Licensor under this Agreement are confidential and proprietary information relating to this Agreement and the business of Licensor and Licensee. Accordingly, the parties agree that each of them shall keep that information confidential and shall not disclose it, or permit it to be disclosed, to any third party (other than to agents or representatives who need to know such information). Licensor shall have the right, however, to disclose that Licensor and Licensee have entered into this Agreement, the royalty rate(s) set forth in this Agreement, that Licensee is paying for Past Products, and that Licensee has consented to the validity, enforceability, and infringement of the Licensed Patents.

4. INDEMNIFICATION

4.1 Licensee Indemnification. Licensee shall at all times during the term of this Agreement and thereafter indemnify, defend, and hold Licensor, its directors, officers, employees, and affiliates, harmless against all claims, proceedings, demands, and liabilities of any kind whatsoever, including legal expenses and reasonable attorneys' fees, arising out of the death of or injury to any person or out of any damage to property, or resulting from the production, manufacture, sale, use, lease, or advertisement of Licensed Products or Past Products or arising from any obligation of Licensee under this Agreement.

4.2 Licensor Indemnification. Licensor shall at all times during the term of this Agreement and thereafter indemnify, defend, and hold Licensee, its directors, officers, employees, and affiliates, harmless against all claims, proceedings, demands, and liabilities of any kind whatsoever, including legal expenses and reasonable attorneys' fees, arising out of any breach of any representation, warranty, or covenant expressly made by Licensor in this Agreement.

5. TERMINATION

5.1 Termination by Licensor. In addition to all other remedies Licensor may have, Licensor may terminate this Agreement and the licenses granted in this Agreement in the event that:

(a) Licensee defaults in its payment to Licensor and such default continues unremedied for a period of thirty (30) days after the Effective Date of this Agreement;

(b) Licensee fails to perform any material obligation, warranty, duty, or responsibility or is in default with respect to any term or condition undertaken by Licensee hereunder, and such failure or default continues unremedied for a period of thirty (30) days after written notice thereof to Licensee by Licensor;

(c) Licensee is liquidated or dissolved;

(d) Any assignment is made of Licensee's business for the benefit of creditors;

(e) Licensee liquidates a substantial portion of its business or engages in a distress sale of substantially all of its assets;

(f) A receiver, or similar officer, is appointed to take charge of a substantial part of Licensee's assets;

(g) Licensee is unable to pay its debts as they mature; or

(h) Any petition in bankruptcy is filed by or against Licensee that remains undischarged for sixty (60) days.

5.2 Termination by Licensee. If all the Licensed Patents are determined to be invalid or unenforceable by any court or tribunal of competent jurisdiction, and the determination becomes final in that it is not further reviewable through appeal or exhaustion of all permissible petitions or applications for rehearing or review, Licensee may terminate this Agreement at will and shall have no further obligations hereunder.

5.3 Effect of Termination. After the termination of this Agreement, Licensee shall have no rights under the Licensed Patents.

5.4 No Discharge on Termination. No termination of this Agreement for any reason shall relieve or discharge either Licensor or Licensee from any duty, obligation, or liability that was accrued as of the date of the termination (including, without limitation, the obligation to indemnify or to pay any amounts owing as of the date of termination).

6. REPRESENTATIONS AND WARRANTIES OF LICENSOR

6.1 Right to Grant License. Licensor represents and warrants that Licensor has the right and authority to grant the licenses granted to Licensee in this Agreement and that this Agreement and the licenses granted in this Agreement do not and will not conflict with the terms of any agreement to which Licensor is a party.

6.2 Disclaimers. Except as otherwise expressly set forth in this Agreement, Licensor, its directors, officers, employees, and agents make no representations and extend no warranties of any kind, either express or implied. In particular, and without limitation, nothing in this Agreement shall be construed as:

(a) a warranty or representation by Licensor as to the validity or scope of the Licensed Patents;

(b) a warranty or representation by Licensor that anything made, used, sold, or otherwise disposed of under any license granted in this Agreement is or will be free from infringement of patents of third parties;

(c) an obligation on the part of Licensor to bring or prosecute actions against third parties for infringement of the Licensed Patents or other proprietary rights;

(d) an obligation on the part of Licensor to furnish any manufacturing or technical information;

(e) the granting by implication, estoppel, or otherwise of any licenses or rights under patents other than the Licensed Patents; or

(f) the assumption by Licensor of any responsibilities whatever with respect to use, sale, or other disposition by Licensee or its vendees or transferees of Licensed Products.

6.3 Limitation of Liability. In no event shall Licensor, its directors, officers, employees, and affiliates be liable for incidental or consequential damages of any kind, including economic damage or injury to property and lost profits, regardless of whether Licensor shall be advised, shall have other reason to know, or in fact shall know of the possibility.

7. REPRESENTATIONS AND WARRANTIES OF LICENSEE

Licensee represents and warrants that Licensee has the right and authority to enter into this Agreement and that this Agreement and the exercise of the licenses granted hereunder does not and will not conflict with the terms of any agreement to which Licensee is a party. Except as otherwise expressly set forth in this Agreement, Licensee, its directors, officers, employees, and agents make no representations and extend no warranties of any kind, either express or implied. In particular, and without limitation, nothing in this Agreement shall be construed as an obligation on the part of Licensee to furnish any manufacturing or technical information.

8. RELATIONSHIP OF THE PARTIES

Nothing in this Agreement will be construed to constitute the parties as partners or joint venturers or constitute either party as agent of the other, nor will any similar relationship be deemed to exist between them. Neither party shall hold itself out contrary to the terms of this paragraph, and neither party shall become liable by reason of any representation, act, or omission of the other contrary to the provisions of this paragraph. This Agreement is not for the benefit of any third party and shall not be deemed to give any right or remedy to any such party, whether referred to in this Agreement or not.

9. ASSIGNMENT

9.1 No Assignment. This Agreement, the rights granted to Licensee, and the duties and obligations of Licensee are all personal to Licensee, and Licensee agrees not to sell, assign, transfer, mortgage, pledge, or hypothecate any such rights in whole or in part, or delegate any of its duties or obligations under this Agreement without the prior written consent of Licensor, which shall not be unreasonably withheld. In the context of this provision, "assignment" shall include the transfer of substantially all of the assets of Licensee, or of a majority interest in the voting stock of Licensee, or the merger, consolidation, or reorganization of Licensee with one or more third parties.

9.2 Binding on Successors. This Agreement will inure to the benefit of and be binding upon Licensor, its successors, and assigns.

10. DISPUTE RESOLUTION

10.1 Arbitration of Royalty Disputes.

(a) Any dispute between Licensor and Licensee concerning the amount of royalties payable to Licensor under this Agreement shall be submitted for binding arbitration in accordance with the provisions of this Section 10 and the then-applicable rules of the American Arbitration Association (the "Association"). Judgment upon the arbitration award may be entered in any court of competent jurisdiction.

(b) The power of the arbitrators shall be limited to resolving the specific issues stated by determining the royalties Licensee owes or should receive credit for, if any, under this Agreement. The power of the arbitrators shall not extend to any other matters. All other disputes shall be subject to litigation in a court of competent jurisdiction.

(c) The arbitration panel or tribunal shall consist solely of neutral arbitrators.

(d) The parties agree that arbitration proceedings under this Agreement shall not be stayed on the ground of pending litigation to which either or both of them is a party.

10.2 Remedies.
Except as expressly provided herein, all specific remedies provided for in this Agreement are cumulative and are not exclusive of one another or of any other remedies available in law or equity.

11. LIMITATIONS OF RIGHTS AND AUTHORITY

11.1 Limitation of Rights.
No right or title whatsoever in the Licensed Patents is granted by Licensor to Licensee, or shall be

taken or assumed by Licensee, except as is specifically set forth in this Agreement.

11.2 Limitation of Authority. Neither party shall, in any respect whatsoever, be taken to be the agent or representative of the other party, and neither party shall have any authority to assume any obligation for the other party, or to commit the other party in any way.

12. MISCELLANEOUS

12.1 Computation of Time. The time in which any act provided in this Agreement is to be done shall be computed by excluding the first day and including the last day, unless the last day is a Saturday, Sunday, or legal holiday, and then it shall also be excluded.

12.2 Notices. All notices given in connection with this Agreement shall be in writing and shall be deemed given upon actual receipt by the addressee. Notices shall be personally delivered or sent by telex or facsimile (with prompt confirmation by registered or certified air mail, postage prepaid) or by registered or certified air mail, postage prepaid, addressed to the party to be notified at the following address, or at such other address as the party may designate by notice:

Licensor:

_____

_____

_____

Attention: _____
Phone: _____
Facsimile: _____

Licensee:

_____

_____

_____

Attention: _____

Phone: _____

Facsimile: _____

12.3 Survival. The provisions of this Agreement relating to payment obligations, confidentiality, indemnification, remedies, and arbitration shall survive the expiration or termination of this Agreement.

12.4 Severability. If any provision of this Agreement is declared by a court of competent jurisdiction to be invalid, illegal, unenforceable, or void, then both parties shall be relieved of all obligations arising under such provision, but only to the extent that such provision is invalid, illegal, unenforceable, or void. If the remainder of this Agreement is capable of substantial performance, then each provision not so affected shall be enforced to the extent permitted by law.

12.5 Waiver and Modification. No modification of any of the terms of this Agreement will be valid unless in writing and signed by both parties. No waiver by either party of a breach of this Agreement will be deemed a waiver by such party of any subsequent breach.

12.6 Headings. The headings in this Agreement are for reference only and shall not in any way control the meaning or interpretation of this Agreement.

12.7 Interpretation. No provision of this Agreement is to be interpreted for or against any party because that party or its attorney drafted the provision.

12.8 Governing Law. This Agreement shall be construed, governed, interpreted, and applied in accordance with the laws of the State of _____.

12.9 No Other Agreement. The parties each represent that in entering into this Agreement, they rely on no promise, inducement, or other agreement not expressly contained in this Agreement; that they have read this Agreement and discussed it thoroughly with their respective legal counsel; that they understand all of the provisions of this Agreement and intend to be bound by them; and that they enter into this Agreement voluntarily.

12.10 Entire Agreement. This Agreement constitutes the complete and exclusive statement of the terms and conditions between the parties, which supersedes and merges all prior proposals, understandings and all other agreements, oral and written, between the parties relating to the subject of this Agreement.

12.11 Counterparts. This Agreement may be executed in counterparts, which taken together shall constitute one document.

IN WITNESS WHEREOF, the parties have executed this Agreement by their duly authorized representatives.

For and on behalf of
[Licensor]

_____ Date: _____, 20____

By: _____

Title: _____

For and on behalf of
[Licensee]

_____ Date: _____, 20____

By:_____

Title: _____

Software (End User) License Agreement[*]

IMPORTANT: READ THIS AGREEMENT CAREFULLY. BY CLICKING ON THE "ACCEPT" BUTTON, OR BY INSTALLING, COPYING, RUNNING, OR OTHERWISE USING THE SOFTCO SOFTWARE, YOU AGREE TO BE BOUND BY THE TERMS OF THIS LICENSE AGREEMENT. IF YOU DO NOT AGREE TO THE TERMS OF THIS LICENSE AGREEMENT, PLEASE CLICK THE "CANCEL" BUTTON, AND DO NOT INSTALL, RUN, COPY, OR OTHERWISE USE THE SOFTCO SOFTWARE.

This End User License Agreement ("License") is a legal agreement between you and SoftCo, Inc., Street, City, State ZIP, USA ("SOFTCO") concerning your use of the SOFTCO Software, together with any electronic documentation that may be provided therewith (collectively, "the Software") through the Software. YOU HEREBY AGREE, BOTH ON YOUR OWN BEHALF AND AS AN AUTHORIZED REPRESENTATIVE OF ANY ORGANIZATION FOR WHICH YOU ARE USING THE SOFTWARE ("EMPLOYER"), THAT YOU AND THE EMPLOYER WILL USE THE SOFTWARE ONLY IN ACCORDANCE WITH THE FOLLOWING TERMS:

1. Disclaimer of Warranty. You expressly acknowledge and agree that use of the Software is at your sole risk. THE SOFTWARE IS PRO-

---

[*] Note: This document is presented for illustrative purposes only. The reader is strongly encouraged to consult with a professional before entering into any license or other contract.

VIDED "AS IS," WITH ALL FAULTS AND WITHOUT WARRANTY OF ANY KIND. SOFTCO does not warrant that the functions contained in the Software will meet your requirements or those of the Employer, or that the operation of the Software will be uninterrupted or error-free, or that defects in the Software will be corrected. Furthermore, SOFTCO does not warrant or make any representation regarding the use or the results of the use of the Software (including the related documentation) in terms of their correctness, accuracy, reliability, or otherwise. Should the Software prove defective, you (and not SOFTCO) assume the entire cost of all necessary servicing, repair, or correction.

★★SOFTCO EXPRESSLY DISCLAIMS ANY WARRANTY OF MERCHANTABILITY, FITNESS FOR A PARTICULAR PURPOSE, TITLE, OR NONINFRINGEMENT WITH RESPECT TO THE SOFTWARE.★★

The Software may be provided with third-party plug-ins or other third-party software, or this Software may be provided as a plug-in for or otherwise in association with third-party software. Use of any such third-party software will be governed by the applicable license agreement, if any, with such third party.

★SOFTCO IS NOT RESPONSIBLE FOR ANY THIRD-PARTY SOFTWARE AND WILL HAVE NO LIABILITY OF ANY KIND FOR YOUR USE OF SUCH THIRD-PARTY SOFTWARE AND MAKES NO WARRANTY OF ANY KIND WITH RESPECT TO SUCH THIRD-PARTY SOFTWARE.★

SOME JURISDICTIONS DO NOT ALLOW THE EXCLUSION OR LIMITATION OF IMPLIED WARRANTIES, SO THE ABOVE EXCLUSIONS MIGHT NOT APPLY TO YOU.

2. Limitation of Liability. In no event will SOFTCO's total liability for all damages exceed the amount of fifty dollars ($50.00).

UNDER NO CIRCUMSTANCES, INCLUDING NEGLIGENCE, WILL SOFTCO BE LIABLE FOR ANY INCIDENTAL, SPECIAL, INDIRECT, PUNITIVE, OR CONSEQUENTIAL DAMAGES, INCLUDING LOST DATA, LOST REVENUE, OR LOST PROFITS, ARISING OUT OF OR RELATING TO THIS LICENSE OR THE SOFTWARE.

SOME JURISDICTIONS DO NOT ALLOW THE EXCLUSION OR LIMITATION OF CONSEQUENTIAL OR INDIRECT DAMAGES, SO THE ABOVE LIMITATION MAY NOT APPLY TO YOU.

3. License Grant. SOFTCO grants to you, and you accept, a personal, nonexclusive, nontransferable license to install and use the Software in object code format at a single site. You may make one copy of the Software in machine-readable form for backup purposes only. The backup copy must include all copyright information contained on the original. This License is effective until terminated as provided below. You may terminate this License by destroying the Software and any copies of the Software in your possession. This License will terminate automatically upon any violation of its terms by you or the Employer. You acknowledge that this License does not entitle you to any support, maintenance, or upgrade from SOFTCO.

4. License Restrictions. You may not do any of the following yourself, or through any third party, and you may not permit any third party with whom you have a business relationship to do any of the following: (A) copy the Software, except as expressly set forth in paragraph 3 above; (B) modify or create derivative works based upon the Software; (C) decompile, disassemble, or reverse engineer the Software in whole or in part; (D) defeat, disable, or circumvent any protection mechanism related to the Software; (E) sell, license, sublicense, lease, or rent, to any third party, whether for profit or without charge, any portion of the Software, or, in particular, without limiting the generality of the foregoing, distribute the Software on any media; make the Software accessible to the public or third parties, whether over networks, electronic bulletin boards, websites, or otherwise; or allow any third party to use the Software except for purpose of your internal business; (F) publish or otherwise communicate any review of or information about the performance of the Software to any third party without the prior written consent of SOFTCO; (G) export, re-export, download, or otherwise use the Software in violation of any laws or regulations, including U.S. Department of Commerce Export Administration regulations and other applicable laws; or (H) use the Software in connection with life support systems, human implantation, medical devices, nuclear facilities, nuclear systems or weapons, aviation, mass transit, or any application where failure or malfunction could lead to possible loss of life or catastrophic property damage.

5. Title and Ownership. This software is protected by United States Patent, Copyright Law and International Treaty provisions. Except for the rights expressly granted above, this License transfers to you no right, title, or interest in the Software, or any copyright, patent, trademark, trade secret, or other intellectual property or proprietary right in the Software. SOFTCO retains sole and exclusive title to all portions of the Software and any copies thereof, and you hereby assign to SOFTCO all right, title, and interest in and to any modifications you make to the Software, whether or not such modifications are permitted. You agree not to disclose the Software to anyone.

6. Export Law Assurances. You may not export, re-export, download, or otherwise use the Software except as authorized by United States law and the laws of the jurisdiction in which it is obtained.

7. Notice to Government End Users. The Software, including any documentation, is provided to the United States Government with restricted rights. If the Software is supplied to the United States Government, the Software is classified as "restricted computer software" as defined in clause 52.227-19 of the FAR. The United States Government's rights to the Software are as provided in clause 52.227-19 of the FAR.

8. Controlling Law and Severability. This License will be governed by the laws of the United States and the State of _____, without regard to their provisions regarding conflicts of laws. This License will not be governed by the United Nations Convention on Contracts for the International Sale of Goods, the application of which is expressly excluded. You irrevocably submit to the jurisdiction of the state and federal courts sitting in _____, and any action or proceeding arising out of this License will be heard and determined in such court. If for any reason a court of competent jurisdiction finds any provision, or portion thereof, to be unenforceable, such provision will be interpreted in order to give effect to such provision to the maximum extent permitted by law, and the remainder of this License will continue in full force and effect.

9. Complete Agreement. This License constitutes the entire agreement between the parties with respect to the use of the Software and supersedes all prior or contemporaneous understandings regarding such subject matter. No amendment to or modification of this License will be binding unless in writing and signed by SOFTCO.

BY CLICKING ON THE "ACCEPT" BUTTON, OR BY INSTALLING, COPYING, RUNNING, OR OTHERWISE USING THE SOFTCO SOFTWARE, YOU AGREE TO BE BOUND BY THE TERMS OF THIS AGREEMENT. IF YOU DO NOT AGREE TO THE TERMS OF THIS AGREEMENT, PLEASE CLICK THE "CANCEL" BUTTON, AND DO NOT INSTALL, RUN, COPY, OR OTHERWISE USE THE SOFTCO SOFTWARE.

Copyright License Agreement[*]

This AGREEMENT is entered into this _____ day of _____,
20___, by and between _____ ("Licensor") and
_____ ("Licensee").

RECITALS

A. Licensor owns the copyright in and to the work entitled
   "_____" (hereinafter "Material").

B. Licensee desires to obtain the rights to incorporate portions of the
   Material into one (1) new work (hereinafter "Work").

NOW, THEREFORE, in consideration of the promises, conditions,
covenants, and warranties herein contained, the parties agree as follows:

1. Rights Granted

Licensor hereby grants to Licensee, its successors and assigns, an exclusive right, license, and privilege worldwide (the "Territory") to:

a. incorporate the Material into the Work and reproduce, distribute, import, and sell the Work throughout the Territory;

---

[*] Note: This document is presented for illustrative purposes only. The reader is strongly encouraged to consult with a professional before entering into any license or other contract.

b. utilize the phrase "incorporating excerpts from [ ]" on or in connection with the packaging, advertising, publicizing, marketing, and distribution of the Work; and

c. utilize and authorize others to utilize the Work (and those portions of the Material incorporated therein) in connection with the advertising, publicizing, marketing, distribution, and use of the Work.

2. Licensor's Rights and Obligations

a. Licensor warrants and represents that it owns all right, title, and interest in and to the Material.

b. Licensor reserves unto itself all rights of every kind and nature except those specifically granted to Licensee herein; provided that Licensor shall not grant any rights to use the Material or any portion thereof in any other work without Licensee's written consent, unless Licensee fails to release the Work to the public on or before [date].

3. Licensee's Rights and Obligations

a. Licensee shall be solely responsible for providing all funding and technical expertise for the development and marketing of the Work.

b. Licensee shall be the sole owner of the Work and all proprietary rights in and to the Work; except, such ownership shall not include ownership of the copyright in and to the Material or any other rights to the Material not specifically granted in Section 1 above.

4. Payments

a. For the rights granted by Licensor herein, Licensee shall pay to Licensor a royalty calculated as follows:

[ ] per unit on the first [ ] units of the Work sold by Licensee.

[ ] per unit on the next [ ] units of the Work sold by Licensee.

[ ] per unit on all sales of the Work over [ ] units.

These royalties are based upon a suggested retail price for the Work of US$_____ and will be adjusted up or down on a pro rata basis should the suggested retail price of the Work change. However, under no circumstances shall royalties to Licensor be less than [ ] per unit.

b. Licensee shall pay to Licensor [ ] on the signing of this Agreement as an advance against the royalties set forth in Section 4.a above.

c. Licensee shall render to Licensor on a quarterly basis, within forty-five (45) days after the end of each calendar quarter during which the Work is sold, a written statement of the royalties due to Licensor with respect to such Work. Such statement shall be accompanied by a remittance of the amount shown to be due. Licensor shall have the right, upon reasonable request, to review those records of Licensee necessary to verify the royalties paid. Any such audit will be conducted at Licensor's expense and at such times and in such a manner as to not unreasonably interfere with Licensee's normal operations. If a deficiency is shown by such audit, Licensee shall immediately pay that deficiency.

5. Warranty and Indemnification

a. Licensor warrants and represents that it has the full right, power, and authority to enter into this Agreement and to grant the rights granted herein; that it has not previously licensed the rights to the Material to any third party; and that Licensee's inclusion and use of the Material will not violate any rights of any kind or nature whatsoever of any third party. Licensor shall indemnify and hold harmless

Licensee, its successors, assigns, and licensees, and the respective officers, directors, agents, and employees, from and against any and all claims, damages, liabilities, costs, and expenses (including reasonable attorneys' fees), arising out of or in any way connected with any breach of any representation or warranty made by Licensor herein.

b. Licensee shall indemnify and hold harmless Licensor, its successors, assigns, and licensees, and the respective officers, directors, agents, and employees, from and against any and all claims, damages, liabilities, costs, and expenses (including reasonable attorneys' fees), arising out of or in any way connected with any claim that the Work infringes any intellectual property rights or other rights of any third party, except to the extent such claim arises from a breach by Licensor of Section 5.a above.

6. Term and Termination

a. The term of this Agreement shall be fifteen (15) years from the date of execution by both parties, unless terminated earlier pursuant to this section.

b. This Agreement shall be subject to termination at the election of Licensor, in the event that Licensee fails to begin distributing Work within one (1) year of the date on which all parties have signed this Agreement, by written notice given by Licensor to Licensee within thirty (30) days of the running of that one- (1-) year period.

c. This Agreement shall be subject to termination at the election of Licensor, by written notice to Licensee, where there has been a default in the due observance or performance of any material covenant, condition, or agreement herein by Licensee, and such default has continued for a period of thirty (30) days after written notice specifying the same shall have been given to Licensor.

d. This Agreement shall be subject to termination at the election of Licensee, by written notice to Licensor, where there has been a default in the due observance or performance of any material covenant, condition, or agreement herein by Licensor and such default has continued for a period of thirty (30) days after written notice specifying the same shall have been given to Licensee.

e. Upon termination or expiration of this Agreement, Licensee shall cease reproducing, advertising, marketing, and distributing the Work as soon as is commercially feasible. Notwithstanding the foregoing, Licensee shall have the right to fill existing orders and to sell off existing copies of the Work then in stock, provided the sell-off period shall not exceed six (6) months from the date of termination. Licensor shall have the right to verify the existence and validity of the existing orders and existing copies of the Work then in stock upon reasonable notice to Licensee.

f. Termination or expiration of this Agreement shall not extinguish any of Licensee's or Licensor's obligations under this Agreement (including, but not limited to, the obligation to pay royalties) which by their terms continue after the date of termination or expiration.

7. General Provisions

a. Successors/Assigns

This Agreement is binding upon and shall inure to the benefit of the respective successors and/or assigns of the parties hereto.

b. Integration

This Agreement sets forth the entire agreement between the parties with respect to the subject matter hereof, and may not be modified or amended except by written agreement executed by the parties hereto.

c. Governing Law: Forum

This Agreement shall be governed by the laws of the State of
_____, applicable to agreements made and to be wholly per-
formed therein.

d. Notice

The address of each party hereto as set forth below shall be the
appropriate address for the mailing of notices, checks, and statements, if any, hereunder. All notices shall be sent certified or registered mail and shall not be deemed received or effective unless and
until actually received. Either party may change their mailing
address by written notice to the other.

IN WITNESS WHEREOF, the parties have caused this License
Agreement to be executed the day and year set forth above.

[Name and address of Licensor]

By: _____

Title: _____

[Name and address of Licensee]

By: _____

Title: _____

Technology License Agreement*

This AGREEMENT is between _____ ("Licensor"), whose address is _____, and _____, a _____ corporation having a principal place of business located at _____ ("Licensee").

RECITALS

WHEREAS, Licensor owns certain Technology Rights related to Licensed Subject Matter; and

WHEREAS, Licensee wishes to obtain a license from Licensor to practice Licensed Subject Matter.

NOW, THEREFORE, in consideration of the mutual covenants and premises herein contained, the parties agree as follows:

1. Effective Date

This Agreement is effective _____ ("Effective Date").

---

* Note: This document is presented for illustrative purposes only. The reader is strongly encouraged to consult with a professional before entering into any license or other contract.

2. Definitions

As used in this Agreement, the following terms have the meanings indicated:

2.1 "Affiliate" means any business entity more than 50% owned by Licensee, any business entity which owns more than 50% of Licensee, or any business entity that is more than 50% owned by a business entity that owns more than 50% of Licensee.

2.2 "Licensed Field" means _____.

2.3 "Licensed Product" means any product Sold by Licensee comprising Licensed Subject Matter pursuant to this Agreement.

2.4 "Licensed Subject Matter" means inventions and discoveries considered to be proprietary know-how or Technology Rights which are within Licensed Field.

2.5 "Licensed Territory" means the _____.

2.6 "Net Sales" means the gross revenues received by Licensee from the Sale of Licensed Products less sales and/or use taxes actually paid, import and/or export duties actually paid, outbound transportation prepaid or allowed, and amounts allowed or credited due to returns (not to exceed the original billing or invoice amount).

2.7 "Sale or Sold" means the transfer or disposition of a Licensed Product for value to a party other than Licensee.

2.8 "Technology Rights" means Licensor's rights in technical information, know-how, processes, procedures, compositions, devices, methods, formulas, protocols, techniques, software, designs, drawings, or data created by _____ ("Inventor") before the Effective Date relating to _____.

3. Warranty: Superior-Rights

3.1 Licensor represents and warrants its belief that (i) it is the owner of the entire right, title, and interest in and to Licensed Subject Matter; (ii) it has the sole right to grant licenses thereunder; and (iii) it has not knowingly granted licenses thereunder to any other entity that would restrict rights granted to Licensee except as stated herein.

3.2 Licensee understands and acknowledges that Licensor, by this Agreement, makes no representation as to the operability or fitness for any use, safety, efficacy, ability to obtain regulatory approval, and/or breadth of the Licensed Subject Matter.

3.3 Licensee, by execution hereof, acknowledges, covenants, and agrees that it has not been induced in any way by Licensor to enter into this Agreement, and further warrants and represents that (i) it has conducted sufficient due diligence with respect to all items and issues pertaining to this Article 3 and all other matters pertaining to this Agreement; and (ii) Licensee has adequate knowledge and expertise, or has utilized knowledgeable and expert consultants, to adequately conduct the due diligence, and agrees to accept all risks inherent herein.

4. License

4.1 Licensor hereby grants to Licensee a royalty-bearing, exclusive license under Licensed Subject Matter to manufacture, have manufactured, and/or sell Licensed Products within the Licensed Territory for use within Licensed Field. This grant is subject to the payment by Licensee to Licensor of all consideration as provided herein.

4.2 Licensee may extend the license granted herein to any Affiliate if the Affiliate consents to be bound by this Agreement to the same extent as Licensee.

4.3 Licensee may grant sublicenses consistent with this Agreement if Licensee is responsible for the operations of its sublicensees relevant to this Agreement as if the operations were carried out by Licensee, including the payment of royalties, whether or not paid to Licensee by a sublicensee. Licensee must deliver to Licensor a true and correct copy of each sublicense granted by Licensee, and any modification or termination thereof, within 30 days after execution, modification, or termination. When this Agreement is terminated, all existing sublicenses granted by Licensee must be assigned to Licensor.

5. Payments and Reports

5.1 In consideration of rights granted by Licensor to Licensee under this Agreement, Licensee will pay Licensor the following:

a. A nonrefundable license documentation fee in the amount of $_____, due and payable when this Agreement is executed by Licensee;

b. An annual license reissue fee in the amount of $_____, due and payable on each anniversary of the Effective Date beginning on the first anniversary;

c. A running royalty equal to _____% of Net Sales for Licensed Products; and

d. A minimum yearly royalty of $_____.

5.2 During the term of this Agreement, and for one (1) year thereafter, Licensee agrees to keep complete and accurate records of its and its sublicensees' Sales and Net Sales of Licensed Products under the license granted in this Agreement in sufficient detail to enable the royalties payable hereunder to be determined. Licensee agrees to permit Licensor or its representatives, at Licensor's expense, to periodically examine its books, ledgers, and records during regular business hours for the purpose of, and to the extent necessary, for verification of any report required under this Agreement. If the amounts due to Licensor are determined to have been underpaid, Licensee will pay the cost of the examination and accrued interest at the highest allowable rate.

5.3   Within thirty (30) days after March 31, June 30, September 30, and December 31, beginning immediately after the Effective Date, Licensee must deliver to Licensor a true and accurate written report, even if no payments are due Licensor, giving the particulars of the business conducted by Licensee and its sublicensee(s), if any exist, during the preceding three (3) calendar months under this Agreement as are pertinent to calculating payments hereunder. This report will include at least:

a. the quantities of Licensed Subject Matter that it has produced;

b. the total Sales;

c. the calculation of royalties thereon; and

d. the total royalties computed and due Licensor.

Simultaneously with the delivery of each report, Licensee must pay to Licensor the amount, if any, due for the period of each report.

5.4   All amounts payable here by Licensee must be paid in United States funds without deductions for taxes, assessments, fees, or charges of any kind. Checks must be payable to Licensor.

6. Term and Termination

6.1   The term of this Agreement is from the Effective Date for a period of _____ years.

6.2   Any time after two (2) years from the Effective Date, Licensor has the right to terminate the exclusivity of this license in any national political jurisdiction in the Licensed Territory if Licensee, within 90 days after receiving written notice from Licensor of intended termination of exclusivity, fails to provide written evidence satisfactory to Licensor that Licensee or its sublicensees has commercialized or is actively attempting to commercialize a licensed invention in such jurisdiction(s).

6.3 Any time after three (3) years from the Effective Date, Licensor has the right to terminate this license in any national political jurisdiction in the Licensed Territory if Licensee, within ninety (90) days after receiving written notice from Licensee of intended termination, fails to provide written evidence satisfactory to Licensor that Licensee or its sublicensees has commercialized or is actively attempting to commercialize a licensed invention in such jurisdiction(s).

6.4 The following definitions apply to Article 6: (i) "Commercialize" means having Sales of Licensed Products in such jurisdiction; and (ii) "Active attempts to commercialize" means having Sales of Licensed Products or an effective, ongoing and active research, development, manufacturing, marketing, or sales program as appropriate, directed toward obtaining regulatory approval, production, or Sales of Licensed Products in any jurisdiction, and plans acceptable to Licensee, in its sole discretion, to commercialize licensed inventions in the jurisdiction(s) that Licensor intends to terminate.

6.5 This Agreement will earlier terminate:

a. automatically if Licensee becomes bankrupt or insolvent and/or if the business of Licensee is placed in the hands of a receiver, assignee, or trustee, whether by voluntary act of Licensee or otherwise; or

b. upon thirty (30) days' written notice from Licensor if Licensee breaches or defaults on its obligation to make payments (if any are due) or reports, in accordance with the terms of Article 5, unless, before the end of the thirty- (30-) day period, Licensee has cured the default or breach and so notifies Licensor, stating the manner of the cure; or

c. upon thirty (30) days' written notice if Licensee breaches or defaults on any other obligation under this Agreement, unless, before the end of the thirty- (30-) day period, Licensee has cured the default or breach and so notifies Licensor, stating the manner of the cure; or

d. at any time by mutual written agreement between Licensee and Licensor, upon one hundred eighty- (180-) days' written notice to all parties and subject to any terms herein which survive termination; or

e. under the provisions of Paragraphs 6.2 and 6.3 if invoked.

6.6 If this Agreement is terminated for any cause:

a. nothing herein will be construed to release either party of any obligation matured prior to the effective date of the termination;

b. after the effective date of the termination, Licensee may sell all Licensed Products and parts therefor it has on hand at the date of termination, if it pays earned royalties thereon according to the terms of Article 5; and

c. Licensee will be bound by the provisions of Articles 8 (Indemnification), 9 (Use of Licensor and Component's Name), and 10 (Confidential Information and Publication) of this Agreement.

7. Assignment

Except in connection with the sale of substantially all of Licensee's assets to a third party, this Agreement may not be assigned by Licensee without the prior written consent of Licensor, which will not be unreasonably withheld.

8. Indemnification

Licensee agrees to hold harmless and indemnify Licensor, its officers, employees, and agents from and against any claims, demands, or causes of action whatsoever, including without limitation those arising on account of any injury or death of persons or damage to property caused by, or arising out of, or resulting from, the exercise or practice of the license granted hereunder to Licensee, its Affiliates, or their officers, employees, agents, or representatives.

9. Use of Licensor and Component's Name

Licensee may not use the name of Licensor without express written consent.

10. Confidential Information and Publication

10.1 Licensor and Licensee each agree that all information contained in documents marked "confidential" and forwarded to one by the other (i) be received in strict confidence, (ii) be used only for the purposes of this Agreement; and (iii) not be disclosed by the recipient party, its agents or employees without the prior written consent of the other party, except to the extent that the recipient party can establish competent written proof that such information:

a. was in the public domain at the time of disclosure;

b. later became part of the public domain through no act or omission of the recipient party, its employees, agents, successors, or assigns;

c. was lawfully disclosed to the recipient party by a third party having the right to disclose it;

d. was already known by the recipient party at the time of disclosure;

e. was independently developed by the recipient; or

f. was required by law or regulation to be disclosed.

10.2 Each party's obligation of confidence hereunder shall be fulfilled by using at least the same degree of care with the other party's confidential information as it uses to protect its own confidential information. This obligation shall exist while this Agreement is in force and for a period of three (3) years thereafter.

11. Alternate Dispute Resolution

Any dispute or controversy arising out of or relating to this Agreement, its construction, or its actual or alleged breach will be decided by mediation. If the mediation does not result in a resolution of such dispute or controversy, it will be finally decided by an appropriate method of alternate dispute resolution, including, without limitation, arbitration, conducted in the city of _____,
in accordance with the Commercial Dispute Resolution Procedures http://www.adr.org/ rules/commercial_rules.html of the American Arbitration Association. The arbitration panel will include members knowledgeable in the evaluation of _____ technology. Judgment upon the award rendered may be entered in the highest court or forum having jurisdiction, state or federal. The provisions of this Article 11 will not apply to any dispute or controversy as to which

any treaty or law prohibits such arbitration. The decision of the arbitration must be sanctioned by a court of law having jurisdiction to be binding upon and enforceable by the parties.

12. General

12.1 This Agreement constitutes the entire and only agreement between the parties for Licensed Subject Matter and all other prior negotiations, representations, agreements, and understandings are superseded hereby. No agreements altering or supplementing the terms hereof may be made except by a written document signed by both parties.

12.2 Any notice required by this Agreement must be given by pre-paid, first class, certified mail, return receipt requested, addressed in the case of Licensor to:

[Name]
[Address _____]
[_____]
[Attention: _____]
[Fax: _____]
[Phone: _____]

with copies to:

[Name]
[Address]

or in the case of Licensee to:

[Name]
[Address _____]
[_____]
[Attention: _____]
[Fax: _____]
[Phone: _____]

or other addresses as may be given from time to time under the terms of this notice provision.

12.3 Licensee must comply with all applicable federal, state, and local laws and regulations in connection with its activities pursuant to this Agreement.

12.4 This Agreement will be construed and enforced in accordance with the laws of the United States of America and of the State of _____.

12.5 Failure of Licensor to enforce a right under this Agreement will not act as a waiver of that right or the ability to later assert that right relative to the particular situation involved.

12.6 Headings are included herein for convenience only and shall not be used to construe this Agreement.

12.7 If any part of this Agreement is for any reason found to be unenforceable, all other parts nevertheless remain enforceable.

IN WITNESS WHEREOF, parties hereto have caused their duly authorized representatives to execute this Agreement

_____ (LICENSOR)   _____ (LICENSEE)

By: _____   By: _____

Name: _____   Name: _____

Title: _____   Title: _____

Date: _____   Date: _____

Georgia-Pacific Factors

On the question of patent license royalty rates, the leading case is *Georgia-Pacific Corp. v. United States Plywood Corp.*, 318 F. Supp. 1116 [S.D.N.Y. 1970], which lists 15 factors to be considered when determining a rate.

1. The royalties received by the patentee for the licensing of the patent in suit, proving or tending to prove an established royalty.

2. The rates paid by the licensee for the use of other patents comparable to the patent in suit.

3. The nature and scope of the license, as exclusive or non-exclusive; or as restricted or non-restricted in terms of territory or with respect to whom the manufactured product may be sold.

4. The licensor's established policy and marketing program to maintain his patent monopoly by not licensing others to use the invention or by granting licenses under special conditions designed to preserve that monopoly.

5. The commercial relationship between the licensor and licensee, such as whether they are inventor and promoter.

6. The effect of selling the patented specialty in promoting sales of other products of the licensee; that existing value of the invention to the licensor as a generator of sales of his non-patented items; and the extent of such derivative or convoyed sales.

7. The duration of the patent and the term of the license.

8. The established profitability of the product made under the patent, its commercial success, and its current popularity.

9. The utility and advantages of the patented property over the old modes or devices, if any, that had been used for working out similar results.

10. The nature of the patented invention; the character of the commercial embodiment of it as owned and produced by the licensor; and the benefits to those who have used the invention.

11. The extent to which the infringer has made use of the invention; and any evidence probative of the value of that use.

12. The portion of the profit or of the selling price that may be customary in the particular business or in comparable business to allow for the use of the invention or analogous inventions.

13. The portion of the realized profit that should be credited to the invention as distinguished from non-patented elements, the manufacturing process, business risk, or significant features or improvements added by the infringer.

14. The opinion testimony of qualified experts.

15. The amount that a licensor (such as the patentee) and a licensee (such as the infringer) would have agreed upon (at the time the infringement began) if both had been reasonably and voluntarily trying to reach an agreement; that is the amount which a prudent licensee—who desired, as a business proposition, to obtain a license to manufacture and sell a particular article embodying the patented invention—would have been willing to pay as a royalty and yet be able to make a reasonable profit and which amount would have been acceptable by a prudent patentee who was willing to grant a license.

Georgia-Pacific, 318 F. Supp. at 1120.

Agreement to Negotiate a License[*]

This **AGREEMENT** to negotiate a license, effective _____,

_____ ("Effective Date"), is between the _____

("LICENSOR"), whose address is _____,

and _____ ("COMPANY"), located at

_____.

    NOW, THEREFORE, in consideration of the mutual covenants and premises herein contained, the parties agree as follows:

1. The parties wish to set forth the conditions under which they will negotiate a license in good faith for the technology described in Exhibit A ("Technology"), such license to be effective no later than 180 days from the Effective Date (the "Term").

2. During the Term, LICENSOR will not pursue any license agreements relating to the Technology in the field of _____ with any other organization, commercial entity, private business, or individual.

3. LICENSOR and COMPANY will begin to negotiate a license within 30 days after COMPANY'S receipt of the funding or by the end of the Term, whichever is sooner. COMPANY agrees to submit to LICENSOR plans for commercializing the Technology when the negotiations begin.

---

* Note: This document is presented for illustrative purposes only. The reader is strongly encouraged to consult with a professional before entering into any license or other contract.

4. The parties wish to negotiate a license that grants COMPANY a(n) (non-) exclusive, royalty-bearing, worldwide license, with the right to grant sublicenses, to use the Technology to manufacture, have manufactured, use, sell, import, and/or offer for sale licensed products or methods for use within a certain field.

5. This license will include at least the following provisions:

    a. reimbursement to LICENSOR of all domestic and foreign patent expenses to date, if any;

    b payment of an up-front license fee;

    c. payment of a running royalty rate;

    d. diligence requirements for commercializing the Technology; and

    e. indemnification, confidentiality, and publication provisions and other reasonable and customary terms in a license agreement.

6. COMPANY agrees to pay LICENSOR $_____ (the "Fee") due and payable when this Agreement is signed by COMPANY. COMPANY further agrees to reimburse LICENSOR for all patent expenses that become due during the Term.

7. The parties will treat each other's confidential information as follows:

    a. LICENSOR and COMPANY each agree that all information contained in documents marked "confidential" and forwarded to one by the other (1) are to be received in strict confidence, (2) are to be used only for the purposes of this Agreement, and (3) are not to be disclosed by the recipient party, its agents, or employees without the prior written consent of the other party, except to the extent that the recipient party can establish competent written proof that such information:

        1. was in the public domain at the time of disclosure;

        2. later became part of the public domain through no act or omission of the recipient party, its employees, agents, successors, or assigns;

3. was lawfully disclosed to the recipient party by a third party having the right to disclose it;

4. was already known by the recipient party at the time of disclosure;

5. was independently developed by the recipient; or

6. was required by law or regulation to be disclosed.

b. Each party's obligation of confidence hereunder shall be fulfilled by using at least the same degree of care with the other party's confidential information as it uses to protect its own confidential information. This obligation shall exist while this Agreement is in force and for a period of three (3) years thereafter.

c. LICENSOR recognizes and agrees that COMPANY may, from time to time, need to enter into related confidentiality agreements with third parties. COMPANY agrees that confidential information will not be disclosed to third parties unless a confidentiality agreement has been fully executed between COMPANY and the third party. Such confidentiality agreement will be at least as restrictive as the sample agreement set forth in Appendix ___. (See Appendix C on page 135.) COMPANY agrees to provide LICENSOR a copy of all confidentiality agreements within 30 days of their execution.

IN WITNESS WHEREOF, parties hereto have caused their duly authorized representatives to execute this Agreement.

_____ (LICENSOR) _____(COMPANY)

By: _____ By: _____

Name: _____ Name: _____

Date: _____ Date: _____

Epilogue

lthough this book is about licensing in the classical (narrow) sense of the word, the licensing professional would be well advised to take the broader view that licensing is, ultimately, a business venture. Often a more profitable business deal can be structured by way of a joint venture or a strategic alliance. Consider that, based on the 25 percent rule, a licensor in a conventional license stands to receive only a quarter of future profits. Perhaps a greater share of profit can be obtained by structuring a joint venture with a prospective licensee or contributing this technology to a start-up formed around it in exchange for equity. Should the start-up succeed and go public, the stock may be worth much more than the royalties paid under a traditional licensing agreement. Many large corporations pursue this type of technology transfer in lieu of "old-fashioned" licensing.

Licensing is a challenging and exciting game. It can be very profitable. Above all, it is but another example of an overriding principle that by sharing, one can do better than by keeping.

Further Reading

Berman, Bruce, ed. *From Ideas to Assets: Investing Wisely in Intellectual Property.* New York: John Wiley & Sons, Inc., 2001.

Chisum, Donald S., Craig Allen Nard, Herbert F. Schwartz, Pauline Newman, and F. Scott Kieff. *Principles of Patent Law.* New York: Foundation Press, 1998.

Davis, Julie L., and Suzanne S. Harrison. *Edison in the Boardroom.* New York: John Wiley & Sons, Inc., 2000.

Goldscheider, Robert, ed. *Licensing Best Practices: The LESI Guide to Strategic Issues and Contemporary Realities.* Hoboken, NJ: John Wiley & Sons, Inc., 2002.

Parr, Russell L., and Patrick H. Sullivan. *Technology Licensing: Corporate Strategies for Maximizing Value.* New York: John Wiley & Sons, Inc., 1996.

Poltorak, Alexander I., and Paul J. Lerner. *Essentials of Intellectual Property.* Hoboken, NJ: John Wiley & Sons, Inc., 2002.

Rivette, Kevin G., and David Kline. *Rembrandts in the Attic.* Boston: Harvard Business School Press, 2000.

Shulman, Seth. *Owning the Future.* New York: Houghton Mifflin, 1999.

Stewart, Thomas A. *Intellectual Capital, the New Wealth of Organizations.* New York: Doubleday/Currency, 1997.

Sullivan, Patrick H. *Profiting from Intellectual Capital, Extracting Value from Innovation.* New York: John Wiley & Sons, Inc., 1998.

White, Edward P. *Licensing: A Strategy for Profits.* Alexandria, VA: Licensing Executives Society, 1990, 1997.

Index

CPSIA information can be obtained at www.ICGtesting.com
Printed in the USA
BVOW03n1826121115

426880BV00002B/5/P